The EHR Guru

A parable that explains how to implement electronic health records without the techno-babble

by

Morris W. Stemp, *CPA, MBA, CPHIMS*

with

David Russell

Printed in the United States of America
First Printing: July 2011

Additional writing and editing by Jeff Russell and Brandon Hoye
Design by David Reyes

Library of Congress Copyright Registration # 1-620923671
Writers Guild of America Intellectual Property Registry: 1513426
13-digit ISBN: 978-0-9771659-7-1
10-digit ISBN: 0-9771659-7-3

DISCLAIMER: The contents of this Book are intended for general information purposes only. Information contained in this document is not intended to be a substitute for legal advice or to provide legal guidance of any kind whatsoever. If legal advice or other expert assistance is required, the services of a competent professional should be sought.

For additional information visit:

www.StempSystems.com ▫ www.SmythBarnabas.com ▫ www.SuccessWithPeople.com

Dedicated to my Partners
Ben Brukner and Aleem Quadri
The real "Gurus" behind Stemp Systems

In memory of my father
Isay Stemp
who taught me about business, integrity,
and most of all, helping and giving to others

With love to my family, **Sam, Atara, Danny, Gaby**, and **Emily**
and in gratitude to my exceptional team at Stemp
whose names are referenced throughout the book

With appreciation and admiration
to my incredibly supportive twin brother
Dr. Leo Stemp
who directs the Critical Care Unit at
Mercy Medical Center in Springfield, Massachusetts

To **Karen** with whom I enjoy life every day

What People Are Saying About **The EHR Guru**

EHR Guru, Morris Stemp, has written a marvelous, easy to read, roman à clef describing EHR implementation that is a must read for anyone still using paper charts and a darn good read even for those who have been digital for much of the new millennium. Whether you use his services or not, it is worth reading, as it describes the nut and bolts of going and staying digital that even the most committed can't help but enjoy. The book is not an ad for any particular software or hardware but an overview of the process you will have to go through to make the transition to the digital age.

Daniel Mark Siegel, MD, MS (Management and Policy)
Partner, Long Island Skin Cancer and Dermatologic Surgery
Clinical Professor of Dermatology, SUNY Downstate
Director, Procedural Dermatology Fellowship

"Stemp has been our IT Guru for the past 10 years and continually guides us through the complexities of delivering healthcare services, and now Meaningful Use. The EHR Guru is just another way Morris helps doctors understand how technology can improve the experience of their patients… and our bottom line."

Steven Ravins, MD
Managing Partner
Raveco Medical

"I finally read The EHR Guru. I did enjoy it and absolutely related to what Sam was going thru. I actually wish I would have read this as a precursor to starting the implementation of our EHR system. I may have had some insight as to what needed to be done behind the scenes that I had no idea of."

Patricia Wylie-Kennedy, RN, CNA
Senior Vice President
Project Samaritan Health Services, Inc.

"In each EHR implementation I have participated in there have been a number of reluctant staff who, despite being presented with all the benefits of an EHR and a comprehensive implementation plan that addresses all their clinical and operational concerns, were still unsupportive of the project. The EHR Guru uses a unique and creative story format to soothe the underlying emotional concerns that frequently overshadow the overwhelming clinical and operational benefits of an Electronic Health Record. The format makes for a quick, easy read; suitable for all levels and positions. I highly recommend it for any practice that is even contemplating the move to electronic health records."

Neil A. Latman, CPA
Vice President of Financial Reporting
Hudson River HealthCare

"We have been using an EHR for the past 7 years. As early adapters, we have lived through a lot of the problems and received many benefits of having an EHR. As more of my colleagues jump on board, we have become inundated with requests for advice on which EHR to choose and the best way to plan and implement the system. I'm glad the EHR Guru book is now available as it contains all the information I know and I lot I didn't know. It is a much better and thoughtful reference than asking me or any of your colleagues for advice."

Mark Stein, MD
Managing Partner
Advanced Urology

"We have a high-performance, high-volume cardiology practice. Eight years ago, when we first implemented our EHR system, it was difficult to understand all the ways the system could help us. We were pioneers back then. I recommend this book, The EHR Guru, to anyone considering an EHR system. It quickly and easily gets you informed about how an EHR can help your practice, why you should invest in it, and the challenges you might encounter when implementing this technology."

Robert Hendler, MBA
Practice Administrator
Cardiac Specialists

"The EHR Guru is a primer written in story form to gently introduce technology beginners to the overwhelmingly complex structure that makes up the modern paperless medical office. Doctors who are drowning in paper, and doctors who already have EHR systems but don't understand how they work, can start with this quick read to find out what's already happening in the world of medical office technology and how to take steps to get there themselves."

Jessica J. Krant, MD, MPH
Founder
Art of Dermatology

The EHR Guru

Contents

Chapter 1
The Ultimatum

"SAM? SAM BUSHMAN, WHERE ARE YOU? IT'S TIME!" Karen yelled.

"It's not the time that's the problem," Sam mumbled to himself, "it's this place!" Sam was busy trying to organize the supply room at MedOne, the medical group where he was the practice administrator.

Around and above him were half-empty boxes of medical supplies and stacks of charts, labels, forms, and miscellaneous papers that no one wanted to touch. It was like an art project that had started small and grown, box by box, until it formed a mass that challenged the imagination. This was the outcome of years of carefully accumulating information about the group's patients. While most of the relevant and recent patient data resided in the filing cabinets out in the front office, the overflow was moved to any available spot in the supply room.

Retrieving the records in a timely manner was just one of the problems Sam and the admin staff had. Sam knew once he found what he was looking for, deciphering it would be another challenge. Karen's handwriting was terrible, but better than any of the other four partners at the practice.

*　*　*

"SAM! I NEED TO LOCK UP!" Karen Metz was hurriedly reading through a series of coffee-ringed medical reports prior to her departure.

MedOne Orthopedics specialized in orthopedic surgery and physical therapy but catered to a wide range of issues dealing with musculoskeletal problems. Basically, if something hurt when you moved, MedOne knew what to do—and Karen was the best.

She was the senior partner and founder of the practice. After earning her degree at Columbia, she had opened MedOne right away. She loved solving people's problems just as much as she enjoyed studying the human body, and she couldn't wait to get her hands dirty, so to speak. Typically for her, she hadn't done a lot of research, but rather had simply dived in, fixing problems as they arose.

One result of that scattershot approach was the boxes and stacks of papers overflowing the supply room. Although Karen was laser-focused on client needs, even she was aware that the systems and processes used to manage the practice were manual, inefficient, or non-existent. Karen knew in a medical practice, accurate and accessible medical records are the key to an efficient, optimized workflow and the best patient care. She felt that MedOne was still locked out in the cold.

*　　*　　*

"SAM!"

"OKAY OKAY! I'M COMING OUT! DON'T SHOOT!" He put down a particularly vexing stack of charts that made no sense whatsoever and made for the door. As he locked the door to the supply room, he felt someone's eyes burning a hole in his right temple.

Karen started off calmly. "Sam, if I don't leave now, I will miss my flight. If I miss my flight, I will have to reschedule. Do you know how much it costs to reschedule a flight to Hong Kong? And if I miss OSHH, I will operate on both your knees without anesthetic!" Her hands shot down and her foot stomped the floor like a first grader's mid-tantrum.

Sam knew Karen was under a lot of stress. Usually she wouldn't be closing up shop so early in the day, but this trip created an exception. The Orthopedic Symposium of Healthy Healing only happens once every two years. Participants from around the globe are invited to hear prominent physicians speak about topics relating to their specialty. Breakout sessions highlight unique procedures and best practices that had been discovered and implemented since the previous symposium. This year, Karen had been invited to host her own breakout talk. She had never done anything like it before, and she was freaking out.

For the past several days, she had been releasing the stress by pestering Sam, and he was ready to collapse. No matter where he tried to hide, she always found him. He wasn't hiding in order to avoid his work; he was trying to avoid her so he could do his work! With every new request, he whined a little inside as he slumped off to follow her commands. He understood that she needed to prepare for her talk, but don't perfectionists take coffee breaks, too? It seemed as though he could barely pour a packet of sugar in his coffee before he had to search for another chart on Ravins, S. or Whylee, P.

*   *   *

After a quick stop in his office, Sam met Karen by the door. He uttered an apology and something about "just finishing up."

"Fine," Karen said. She and Sam walked out the rear, staff-only exit to the parking lot in silence. Karen knew what she was going to say next—what she had to say—but she was searching for a way to begin.

Sam's protracted excursions into the supply room were nothing new to her. She knew he had been trying to organize it for months. The problem was that for every chart he filed away, four more would arrive to take its place. Sam meant well, but he was clearly overwhelmed by the sheer volume and variety of forms that came flooding in and built themselves into leaning pinnacles of medical deadweight. The time wasted in filing, finding, and deciphering records was costing the practice money and bogging down productivity.

They paused at Karen's car. "Well, good luck, Kar!" Sam said. "Knock 'em dead! Um, I mean, break a leg! Wait, that's not what I mean either. You know what I mean, right?" He shrugged and gave her a sheepish grin.

She smiled, "Yes, I know what you mean, Sam." Then a serious expression came over her face.

"What's up?" Sam looked confused.

"Sam, things have got to change around here. I know you've been working hard, but it's not good enough. We have got to get smart." She paused and took a breath. "This medical practice is drowning in paper, and I'm afraid that you can't handle it alone."

*   *   *

Sam was taken aback. He had not been expecting this. "Whoa, wait a minute. What do you mean? We've been doing alright haven't we? I mean, it's not perfect but we get the job done … eventually." He swallowed hard.

"Sam, I'll put it plainly. We need to be more efficient. I spoke with Kurt Taylor last week about how we can better serve our patients and our staff. He suggested talking with this guy." She handed Sam a business card with a plus sign in between two symbols: the classic medical caduceus, and a power-on button:

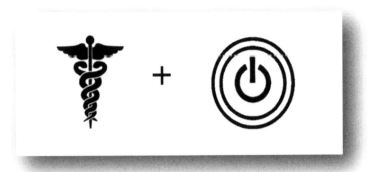

On the back were these words:

The EHR Guru

Giving Power to the Medical Practitioners

Tel. (718) 784-7376   info@theehrguru.com

"Of all the doctors I have spoken with over the past year, Kurt Taylor's practice is the best. And he's a pediatrician! I'm putting tendons and bones back together; all he does is deal with snotty-nosed kids all day! Yet I've heard people say he has the most structured, best managed, efficient medical practice in the state. And I'll bet they NEVER lose any patient records!"

Sam felt as if he'd been punched. "Now hold on. That's—"

"Come on, Sam, how long has it been since we lost Rachel Torres's surgery records? We've been looking for them for three weeks!"

"But—"

"And we still can't get paid by insurance companies on time, not consistently. We need a better system. I want you to get in contact with Kurt Taylor, and talk to this EHR Guru. I know you're not big on technology, but it's time to step up to the plate."

That was an understatement. The mere mention of computers and electronics made Sam's skin crawl. Except for internet surfing and email, he knew next to nothing about technology. Everyone else in the office had a smart phone, but Sam clung to what he called his dumb phone.

Sam could tell that Karen was working up to something big. She always made a point of finishing strong. She opened her car door, and Sam took a deep breath.

"Sam, I've already spoken with the other partners about this. If you don't have a plan for implementing a new system of records and workflow around here by the time I return from this trip ... I'm going to have to fire you."

And with that, she slid into her car and drove away, leaving Sam standing alone, open-mouthed, in the parking lot.

Chapter 2
The Dilemma

Sam had been looking forward to the end of this short day all week. But even though it was three o'clock and he was driving home, he still felt like he was at work. The events of the past hour played over and over in his head. Karen's words had made their mark, as she had clearly intended them to. *If you don't have a plan ... I'm going to have to fire you.* Her ultimatum sounded almost theatrically ominous. Unfortunately, it was now a fact of Sam's life.

"How am I going to figure this one out?" he asked aloud. He glanced at the card she had given him and noticed the name on it: The EHR Guru. *Well, that sounds dumb,* he thought. When Sam thought of a guru, he pictured a candle-lit shrine somewhere in India, with a tiny, white-bearded old man sitting on pillows in the middle of the floor teaching a circle of followers how to achieve enlightenment. *So, an EHR Guru does the same thing, just with computers. Ha!* Sam chuckled to himself as he pictured a wrinkled, old Indian guru and his circle of disciples sitting on computers. He hoped it was that easy.

As he pulled into the driveway, Sam saw that his wife's car was already there. *What is Alina doing home already? Doesn't Kevin have soccer practice?* He hoped there wasn't anything wrong. He preferred only one surprise per day. As he reached into the back seat for his briefcase, he heard a loud coughing sound coming through the open living room windows. *Uh oh. That doesn't sound good.*

He opened the front door and looked in. His son, Kevin, was lying on the couch, covered up to his chin with blankets and barking like a sea lion. Alina was hovering over him with a cold compress in one hand and a cup of water in the other. "Look, Kevin! Daddy's home!" Kevin grinned weakly. Sam was immediately concerned, but he did his best to smile back as he put his briefcase down. He moved over to the couch and sat on the end.

"Hey, pal. How are you feeling?"

"Not so good," Kevin croaked.

Sam looked up at Alina, "How long has he been like this?"

"He had the sniffles this morning, but he seemed okay to go to preschool. I was halfway through my grocery list when Mrs. Byrnes called. Apparently he'd started to play tag with Eli and Ezra, but burst into a coughing fit and had to stop. I picked him up at eleven thirty."

Sam tousled Kevin's hair. "You've been home since eleven thirty? You lucky dog! What have you and Mommy been doing?"

Alina answered for him. "We read books and watched TV until he fell asleep around two. He was even wheezing a bit in his sleep. Your car must have woken him up, and he started coughing again."

She looked worried. Kevin had been sick before, but now his coughing seemed more intense than usual. His face was drawn; his eyes were dull. It did not seem like an ordinary cold to Sam.

"Kevin, Daddy and I need to talk in the kitchen," Alina said. "Do you want me to turn on the TV for a little bit?"

"Yes, please," said Kevin weakly. "Can I watch more Scooby-Doo?"

"Schkoobie doobie doooo!" Sam called from the kitchen in his best Scooby-Doo voice. Kevin giggled.

Sam grabbed some cold chicken from the refrigerator and sat down at the kitchen table. But instead of eating it, he just stared off into space. *This is great,* he thought. *I'm gonna get fired, and my son is going to die from the common cold.*

Alina came in and sat down across from him. She could read him like a children's book. After a minute of her silent questioning, Sam opened up.

"I have to come up with a better system to manage our medical records at work or I'll be fired." He stated it matter-of-factly, and then finally took a bite of his snack.

Alina tried to remain calm, but her eyes widened and she exclaimed, "Oh my gosh! What are you going to do?"

"I don't know." Sam shook his head. "I've been frustrated with the current system for a while—because of how much paperwork we've collected over the years—but I have no idea how to make it better. If I did, I would have made changes a long time ago."

"Is it their system?"

"No, it's mine. I instituted it back at the beginning. I'm used to this system. I learned it when I worked for Dad. There's more paper now because of all the forms and bureaucracy, but other than that, this office is pretty much the same as Dad's office."

Sam's father was a pediatrician in his home town of Seattle. He had given Sam a job every summer and Christmas break from college. It gave Sam a great opportunity to learn the fundamentals of running a medical practice while he was earning his degree in business management at NYU.

After graduating, Sam got a job as an assistant to the practice administrator at a medium-sized medical group in New Jersey. Three years later, two things happened: Sam met Alina, and, a few months later, he heard about a new practice start-up in Sharon, Connecticut, by the name of MedOne. After talking with Alina, he left his job, and they moved to nearby Lakeville so he could serve as the practice administrator for Karen.

"What does Karen say?"

"She says everything is slow and inefficient. She said we're 'drowning in paper.'" Alina gave him a questioning look. "Yes, she's right. We are drowning in paper. But I haven't got a clue about where to find a lifeboat."

"Well, did she give you any hints as to how to go about it? Or did she just dump it all in your lap?"

"No, she just…" he started, but then corrected himself. "Well … yes, she did. She told me to get in contact with a pediatrician in Torrington. Guy named Kurt Taylor." He reached into his pocket. "She also gave me this." He handed Alina the business card.

"The EHR 'Guru'? Oooh, sounds magical." Sam smiled, and Alina patted his shoulder. "I'll take Kevin to his pediatrician tomorrow, and you can go visit your pediatrician."

"Okay, that works for me," said Sam. "Do you want to call for an appointment, or should I?"

"I'll do it." Alina picked up the phone and dialed. After a moment, she said, "Hi, this is Alina Bushman. I'm calling to make an appointment for my son, Kevin. He has a terrible cold and a barking cough. Is Dr. Grant available tomorrow?"

Sam was still sitting at the kitchen table, finishing his chicken. He saw a look of disappointment fall across Alina's face.

"Okay," she said. "Well no, that's okay. I need someone to see him right away." There was another pause, then she grabbed a pen and scribbled something on a note pad. "Okay, I'll do that. Thank you." She hung up the phone and turned to Sam.

"Dr. Grant is out until next Wednesday, but Lindsey suggested we contact either Ruth Rose in Millerton or Kurt Taylor in Torrington, because they're good at handling quick visits. Especially Dr. Taylor." She grinned. "Her words, not mine."

Sam shrugged. "Well, I guess I'll call Dr. Taylor. Maybe I can kill two birds with one sick kid." Alina handed him the phone and the number. A receptionist picked up after the first ring.

"Taylor Pediatrics, this is Tara. How may I help you?"

"Hi, my name is Sam Bushman. I'm calling to see if you have any openings tomorrow to see my son Kevin. He's four, and he has a terrible cold and a barking cough."

"Oh the poor thing," said Tara. "Is he a patient of Dr. Taylor's?"

"No, we usually see Dr. Grant in Sharon. But he's unavailable, and his office referred us to you."

"Well, I have good news. Dr. Taylor is available at ten, and I'm sure he'll know exactly how to help Kevin."

"Really? That was fast!" Sam said. "What do we need to bring as far as medical information, insurance ...?"

"If you give me your email address, I'll set you up on our system so you can pre-register online at home tonight using our patient portal. Or, if you prefer, you can simply register tomorrow morning at our reception kiosk. Either way, please remember to bring Kevin's insurance card and some form of identification so we can confirm who you are."

Sam gave Tara his email address, which she repeated back.

"I've added Kevin as a patient and you as the primary contact on our patient portal. Your temporary password is your first name, Sam, in lowercase letters. You'll be required to change your password the first time you use the system. You should receive an email shortly explaining how to access the system and complete your profile." Tara giggled. "Have you got all that?"

"Yes, I think I do. Thanks."

"One more thing. How long has Kevin been feeling poorly?"

"He's been sniffling a little for the past week, but he just started feeling really bad around lunchtime today." Sam looked at Alina for confirmation, and she nodded.

"Okay, I'll make a note of it in our system for Dr. Taylor," Tara replied. "I've already sent you that e-mail to pre-register. We'll see you tomorrow."

"Okay, thanks! Bye." Sam hung up the phone. "Well, that was almost too easy."

Alina beamed. "They had an opening?"

"Yep." Then his face fell. "I guess I'd better see how complicated this online registration is."

Sam headed toward the computer, and Alina left the kitchen to check on Kevin. When Sam logged onto his email account, he saw the registration message from Tara:

From: Tara Pons <tara@taylorpediatrics.com>
To: sbushman1974@aol.com
Subject: Taylor Pediatrics - Register for Your Appointment

Hello Sam,

Welcome to the Taylor Pediatrics Patient Portal! We are pleased to have an opportunity to serve you and your family.

Please click on the link below to enter our system and follow these steps:

http://www.taylorpediatrics.com/registration/bushman29j38dj

1. Enter your username and password, which are your email address and "sam".

2. You will be required to create a new password. Please do so.

3. You will then be asked to confirm your appointment on Friday, July 28, at 10:00 am. Please do so.

While you are online in our system, please complete your child's patient profile so you do not have to take the time to provide this information when you arrive for your appointment.

You will receive a confirmation email upon completing your patient profile.

Thank you!

Sincerely,

Tara Pons
Patient Care Coordinator
Taylor Pediatrics Group P.C.
tara@taylorpediatrics.com
(860) 555-7376

Sam clicked on the link. After entering the system and changing his password, he was taken to a page where he confirmed the appointment. Next, the system asked him to complete Kevin's online profile. Sam entered the information and clicked "Submit." A message popped up that said he had successfully completed the patient profile and would receive a confirmation via email within five minutes.

He checked on Kevin and Alina, and then returned to the computer. A simple message from Tara was waiting for him:

Thank you for pre-registering for your appointment! Please remember to bring your insurance card and some form of identification, such as a driver's license. We look forward to serving you!

At that moment, Sam realized something: *That was easy. What the heck have I been missing?* He had not used a pen or pencil once while scheduling the appointment. He hadn't done too badly with the technical side of things, either.

That night, Sam kept tossing and turning. Karen's ultimatum kept running through his head. He thought back to the simple, online registration process, and to his experiences hunting for the right chart in the supply room. Finally, ignoring Alina's protests, he got out of bed and went down to the computer.

Chapter 3
The Cure

A simple Google search for "ehr" brought up 16.3 million results, as well as advertisements for a wide variety of EHR software vendors. Sam quickly learned that the acronym "EHR" stands for Electronic Health Record, which is similar to an Electronic Medical Record, "EMR," and to a Patient Health Record, or "PHR." He also discovered that there were over four hundred EHR software vendors in the United States. Just as he felt his head starting to swim, he found an entry on a medical wiki that answered most of his initial questions.

An **Electronic Medical Record** is loosely defined as the legal patient record created in an **EHR/EMR** system, usually in a hospital or ambulatory environment. **EMR** is an evolving concept, but it is usually defined as a systematic collection of electronic health information about individual patients. Its purpose is twofold: it provides a complete record of patient encounters, which allows the automation and streamlining of the workflow in healthcare settings. It also increases safety through evidence-based decision support, quality management, and outcomes reporting.

Such records may include a whole range of data either in comprehensive or summary form, including patient demographics, medical history, medication and allergies, immunization status, laboratory test results, radiology images, vital signs, personal stats like age and weight, and billing information. This data may be gathered through the use of lab and medical equipment interfaces, and by notes entered by nurses, physicians, and other patient caregivers regarding procedures they administered to the patient, along with other observations. Each electronic gathering and input of data is considered an individual medical record attributed to a specific patient.

An **Electronic Health Record** is a collection of all the raw data and medical records possessed by all **EHR**-capable facilities that have interacted with a patient. Recorded in digital format, the **EHR** contains the whole picture regarding a patient's health, and allows doctors and other clinical staff to evaluate multiple pieces of data on a patient from different health care providers in a single place.

Sam thought he was starting to get the picture. He wasn't sure he could handle another acronym, but he wanted to know what distinguished a Patient Health Record from an EHR and an EMR. Again, the wiki came through for him.

A **Patient Health Record** or **PHR** is typically a health record that is initiated and maintained by an individual. An ideal **PHR** would provide a complete and accurate summary of the health and medical history of an individual by gathering data from many sources and making this information accessible online to anyone who has the necessary electronic credentials to view the information.

As Sam continued his research, several things gradually became clear. One was the terms EHR and EMR don't have any hard and fast definitions. Exactly what constitutes an electronic health record and an electronic medical record seems to vary slightly depending on the source. Some sites used "EMR" to refer to a patient's medical data and information, and "EHR" to mean that plus other patient information. Other sites seemed to do exactly the opposite.

Even so, EHR systems offered some clear advantages. One that struck Sam right away was that having a digital record of a patient's charts eliminates the possibility of losing them. There's always a backup. Thinking back to the case of the lost Rachel Torres records gave Sam a fleeting pang of guilt. He was anxious to prevent a similar debacle from happening again.

Sam also realized the scanning of reports means a chart or form will no longer be in danger of death by coffee spill, crying, tearing, or bad weather. Karen's coffee-drinking addiction might lead her to warm up to this idea quickly.

One more thing caught Sam's eye:

Transportability: EMR systems may also facilitate the electronic exchange of patient demographic and insurance data and other patient medical information including allergies, past chief complaints, and procedures if they integrate with an electronic Health Information Exchange or HIE. This information may be transferred using the HIE as a middleman through the use of a common technical format called a CCD or CCR, continuity of care document or record.

Sam didn't even try to follow the HIE/CCD/CCR stuff. But he realized if an EHR system could, in fact, "facilitate the electronic exchange of patient demographic and insurance data and other patient medical information," it would help both him and the practice.

Several patients who were now treated at MedOne had previously gone to other practices. Sam was always amazed at the variety of ways different practices filed their paperwork. Sometimes, this difference in filing habits caused delays when one was trying to retrieve information regarding a patient. Even within MedOne, different doctors recorded information in different ways. Apparently, an EHR eliminates those problems because all patient records are maintained in a similar, standardized fashion.

On a more personal level, Sam realized facilitating the electronic exchange of information would mean less paper for him to deal with. And given that his job was hanging on his ability to manage paper, less was definitely more.

That night, Sam dreamed he was in the MedOne supply room. Medical records, insurance forms, and X-rays were pouring out of the ceiling. They knocked him to the ground and covered him up. He was having trouble breathing. He couldn't see. Then he felt something in his hand. It was a computer mouse. He clicked it, and all the stacks upon stacks of paper were sucked into a computer screen and set into nice, orderly folders.

Chapter 4
V.I.P. Reception

The next morning, Sam walked into Taylor Pediatrics hand-in-hand with a still somewhat lethargic Kevin. He could not help but admire the light, child-friendly attitude of the office. A large Lego building-table sat in the middle of the waiting room, and plenty of coloring books and large, smelly pens and colored pencils were scattered around the floor. There was also a computer kiosk, which Sam assumed was for patient use. As they approached the receptionist, he noticed a small, green T-Rex on top of her desk, with a tiny sign at its feet that read "I'm Tara! Pleased To Eat You!" Kevin laughed when Sam told him what the sign said.

Tara herself was a largish woman in her mid-twenties, with collar-length, dyed-black hair and funky glasses. As soon as she spoke, the word "perky" popped into Sam's head.

"Good morning! You must be Sam,"—he nodded—"and you must be Kevin. Do you like my T-Rex?" Now it was Kevin's turn to nod. Tara reached into her drawer and pulled out another toy just like it. "I have an extra one, and since it's your first time here, you can have it."

Kevin was delighted. He grabbed the dinosaur from her and held it up to admire it.

Sam smiled and gently squeezed his son's shoulder. "What do you say?"

"Thank you," Kevin said, without taking his eyes off the toy.

Sam looked back up at Tara. He opened his mouth to speak, but stopped as the realization hit him: There were no stacks of paper behind her. Typically at a practice of this size, a receptionist's desk looks as if a tornado of medical forms has just ripped through. Tara's desk, however, was a clean expanse of wood-grain plastic, and there wasn't a filing cabinet in sight. Sam took this all in for a moment. Then he realized Tara was patiently waiting for him to return to their conversation.

"So, uhh, I pre-registered for our appointment online last night. Do you need me to fill out any forms?"

"No, but you do need to review this." She handed him a document full of lots of small type. "This is a copy of our privacy policies as required by HIPAA. Once you're done reading it, please sign here to confirm you've reviewed it." She swiveled an electronic signature pad towards him, and he nodded to indicate he understood.

"You registered on our online portal? That's great! So you don't need to use the patient kiosk. I just need your son's insurance card and your driver's license so I can confirm who you are." She smiled apologetically. "It's to protect your privacy."

Sam handed over his driver's license and Kevin's insurance card. Tara looked at the driver's license photo, at Sam, and back at the photo. Then she slid the insurance card through a scanner on the side of her monitor. "Hmm, I don't see any medical history for Kevin. Has he been to any of the other doctors connected to our HIE?"

"He's only been to Dr. Grant. I guess their office isn't connected."

"That's okay. It's never too late to start an electronic history."

Sam glanced over the HIPAA privacy statement and then signed the electronic pad. The office system must have confirmed that their insurance was active, because Tara returned the insurance card and driver's license to him.

Sam didn't want to appear intrusive, but his curiosity got the best of him.

"How do you operate without paper forms?"

"Much easier than we used to! It was really a struggle to keep up with all the paper before we went digital." Tara's enthusiasm for the EHR system was obvious. "Now we scan everything. Our old, paper records are filed away in a storage facility."

"If they've all been scanned in, why are you keeping the originals?"

"One of our doctors is concerned Uncle Sam might have some deep, dark regulation we missed. Or maybe a lawyer will subpoena someone's original, paper records. I'm guessing we'll probably shred them in a few years."

"That sounds nice," Sam sighed. "I work at MedOne in Sharon, and our supp— our file room is like a black hole. Records get sucked in there, but we can't ever get them out again."

She laughed. "We used to have the same problem."

"Does it get complicated when you access all those digitized forms and other patient data only on computers?"

"Oh, no. It's very straightforward. Take a look." She turned her monitor toward Sam. "This is your son's identification information. Depending on where I click," she moved the cursor across the screen, "I can see his appointment history, charts, X-rays, prescriptions, or anything else I want to know."

"Wow, that's ..."

"Awesome? I know! I love it." She turned the monitor back. "I don't know how everything works. I just know it makes my job easier. Dr. Taylor understands the guts of the software. You should ask him about it."

"Oh, trust me, I'm going to," Sam replied.

He took a seat next to Kevin, who was quietly playing with his new toy. Sam was surprised to see that the waiting room was uncrowded. Two tween-aged girls and their mother were reading magazines on a couch in one corner. In another corner, a young father waited with his daughter, who looked to be around Kevin's age. The rest of the two dozen or so seats were empty.

Sam thought about Dr. Grant's waiting room, which always seemed to be packed with sick kids and worried parents. If there were so few patients waiting here, did that mean that Taylor Pediatrics' care was substandard? Why weren't more people trying to get in here?

After a few moments, he got up and walked back to Tara's desk.

"I'm sorry to bother you again."

"No bother at all," she chirped.

"Do you mind if I ask you another professional question?"

"Fire away."

"How many patients do you see in a typical day?"

"Well, with five practitioners, we usually serve between seventy-five and eighty-five patients per day." She saw Sam's reaction and laughed. "I know! Before our EHR system was installed, we could only handle forty-five or fifty patients per day, and the waiting room was always full."

"But how does a computer system allow you to see more patients?"

"Efficiency. We used to waste a lot of time rescheduling a double-booking, or searching for a missing chart. That doesn't happen anymore."

Sam did a quick mental calculation. "And that enabled you to increase your efficiency by fifty percent?"

"Not just that, no. There are other things. For example, the time we save on documentation is enormous! Patients register online, not in the waiting room. They receive electronic reminders—email or texts—and now they mostly arrive on time for their appointments. And get this! The system staggers the appointments to lower the number of people in the waiting room at any given time!"

"Yeah, I'd wondered why it was so empty."

"And don't forget, sometimes patients don't have to come into the office at all."

Sam thought a moment. "Okay, you're going to have to explain that one to me."

"Well, take what happened last night, for example. A woman," Tara narrowed her eyes, "I'm not saying who…"

"Privacy."

"Exactly. She couldn't understand the instructions that came with her child's prescription. Dr. We— I mean, her doctor was out, but the on-call doc logged onto the system from his home, pulled up the baby's EHR, and answered all the woman's questions. Simple as that! So now she doesn't have to come in today. Heck, the doctors can even view X-rays, MRIs, and other information—and give advice—from anywhere in the world, as long as they have an internet connection.

Sam was impressed with everything he'd heard. Before he could return to his seat, a door behind him opened and a nurse came into the room. She carried some type of hand-held electronic device, which made her look like a reporter gathering information for a story. She glanced down at the screen.

"Kevin Bushman?"

Sam turned to her. "Right here." She gave him a questioning look. "Well," he said, "over there, actually. C'mere, pal."

The nurse smiled at Kevin as he approached. "Hi, Kevin. My name is Kayla."

The boy smiled at her. "My name's Kevin."

Sam was trying to get a look at the device she was carrying. "Do you mind if I ask what you're holding?"

"It's okay," Tara piped up. "He's one of us."

Kayla seemed more confused than reassured by that. "It's a tablet computer," she said. Sam sensed that she would not be as receptive to his questions as Tara had been.

Kayla smiled warmly at Kevin and reached for his hand. "Would you please come with me?" Sam followed as she led the boy through the door she'd come in, down a wide hallway, to a scale. She measured Kevin's height and weight, and recorded them on the tablet computer.

Then she took Kevin's hand again and led him to an exam room. It was large, as exam rooms go, with a counter running around two sides, cabinets under most of it, a sink, some shelves, an exam table, and two small rolling stools. Sam noticed appreciatively that it didn't smell like antiseptic or air freshener. Kayla had Kevin hop up on the exam table. She put a large, white clip on the end of his thumb. Sam saw that the cord on the clip was attached to the tablet. When had she connected that? He tried to unobtrusively get a look at the screen.

Kayla took the clip off Kevin's thumb and wrapped a blood-pressure cuff around his arm. The cuff was also connected to the tablet. Sam found the blood-pressure box on the screen, and a moment later, Kevin's reading—90 over 50—appeared in it. A green check mark lit up next to the box. Sam knew that Kevin's reading was within normal limits for his age, and assumed that's what the check mark meant.

Next, Kayla used an ear thermometer to take Kevin's temperature. When the thermometer beeped, she typed the information into the tablet. Then she looked up at Kevin and grinned. "Do you want to see something cool?"

"Yeah," replied Kevin and Sam simultaneously. Kayla stood next to Kevin and showed him the tablet's screen. Sam looked over the boy's shoulder. On the right side of the screen was a line graph. The line sloped upward, and had a big yellow dot near the top.

"See that dot there?" Kayla asked. Kevin nodded. "That's you. You are in the eighty-seventh percentile for kids your age. That means if there were one hundred four-year-old boys here, and we lined them up smallest to biggest, you would be number eighty-seven. You're growing up very, very well." Kevin smiled at that.

Kayla turned to Sam. "Dr. Taylor will be with you in a moment." Sam thanked her as she left the exam room.

Chapter 5
The Exam

Dr. Taylor looked to be in his mid-forties, with a jolly disposition and graying tufts of hair lining his long sideburns that made him look like an aging race-car driver. He was smiling as he entered the exam room and extended his hand to Sam. "I'm Dr. Taylor. Nice to meet you."

Sam shook his hand firmly. "Sam Bushman."

The doctor crouched down to child-level and glanced around the room. "I'm looking for someone named Kevin." He looked at Kevin. "Is that you?"

Kevin nodded and muttered "Uh-huh." He was clutching his new T-Rex friend with both hands.

Dr. Taylor tapped the new toy. "I see you've met Tara! She's pretty cool isn't she? Well, guess what? I can be cool too. I'll prove it to you." He turned and pointed at the counter. Sam wondered when the doctor had put down the small toy triceratops. He didn't think it had been there when they entered the exam room.

"See that triceratops?" Dr. Taylor asked. Kevin nodded emphatically. "Well, he's all yours if you can answer one question: How many horns does a triceratops have?" His hands darted in front of the dinosaur to block Kevin's view.

Of course, Kevin knew the answer anyway. "Three," he replied hoarsely.

"Oh! They always know!" Dr. Taylor handed the triceratops to Kevin. "Here you go, my friend. Good answer!" His smile gave way to a concerned look. "I've heard that you've got a cold and a cough. Is that right?" Kevin nodded.

"He's been like this for the past twenty-four hours," Sam said.

The doctor stood up and reached for a stethoscope. "Yes, I saw that last night when I was reviewing today's schedule. Let's take a closer look and hope for the best."

He spent a full minute listening to Kevin's chest and back. When he took the stethoscope out of his ears, Sam spoke up.

"So, you must stay here pretty late if you review your schedule in the evenings."

"No, I leave around five-thirty most days." He typed as he spoke, and Sam wondered how he managed to avoid typing what he was saying. "I can access the office computer from home. Most nights, after dinner, I take a quick peek at what the next day has in store for me."

"Can you access patient's records from home, too?"

"Sure. If I want to."

"What about emailing the records? Say, if you refer a patient to a specialist?"

Dr. Taylor finished his typing and looked up at Sam. He stared at him for a moment, and then asked, "Are you the fella who works for Karen Metz?"

Sam chuckled. "Well, I'm a fella who works for Karen Metz."

Dr. Taylor began searching through the pockets of his lab coat. "She told me you'd be calling. Why didn't you say so?" He pulled a slip of paper from a pocket and looked at it. "'Sam Bushman.' Ha! That's you! She said you were having problems with … something. Records, was it? Is she giving you a hard time? I'm not surprised. She's a tough cookie."

"Yeah, she is a driver, alright. Here's the thing: I'm the practice administrator at MedOne, and I'm thinking I need to get an EHR system in place there soon. Better than soon. Fast."

"And you're asking me because Karen said we have the answer to your problems. Is that why you came here today?" He looked down at Kevin with an overly stern expression. "Are you even sick, young man?" In response, Kevin coughed several times. "Okay, then I'll continue examining you. Open your mouth wide." He picked up a penlight. "Wide!" He shone the light into Kevin's throat. "Wider!"

For the next several minutes, Dr. Taylor examined Kevin, typed notes into his computer, and talked to Sam, all at the same time. Sam was amazed at the doctor's ability to multitask.

"First of all," he said, "a records problem is not just a records problem. Yes, it affects your patient satisfaction, and it frustrates the doctors. But it could also be creating a legal liability. Had you ever thought of that?"

"Yes," Sam admitted.

"Okay, we're agreed you need to do something. So, second of all, an EHR system is not going to be an instant solution. It's not a quick fix or a magic button."

To Kevin he said, "Open your mouth wide again. Wider." He picked up an otoscope and checked the boy's right ear. "Wider!" He moved to the left ear. "Why is your mouth open? Can't you see I'm checking your ears?" Kevin laughed, but quickly segued into coughing.

"I was a pioneer in the use of electronic health records back in the day," Dr. Taylor continued. "I thought technology was the answer to all of the money I spent on filing cabinets. The first system we bought was supposed to be so great. Wonderful! Amazing! But at first, we couldn't even get the darn thing to work!"

Uh-oh, Sam thought.

"It actually killed our productivity for three months. Zero. Nothing we could do. Why? Well, you can't upgrade from a bike to an airplane if you don't know how to fly, now can you? The vendor installed the system, but they didn't train us how to use it properly. And neither did the technology partner who was supposed to be supporting us."

To Kevin he said, "Open your mouth wide again. Wider!" He tested the boy's reflexes with a rubber hammer. "Wider, I say!" But Kevin couldn't keep his mouth open. He was laughing too hard.

"So, after several months of frustration, I finally called the president of the EHR Company and demanded help. She referred me to the 'Guru of electronic health record systems implementations and support.'"

Sam was getting used to hearing that name.

"I thought it was a joke. Still, this EHR Guru was their top outside consultant at the time. I think he still is their go-to guy.

"Personally, I like to stay with my current vendors. But the technology partner was not helping us grow. They were holding us back. It was costing us a lot of money in terms of lost productivity. So we gave the Guru a call."

He finished with the computer tablet and set it down on the counter. "Okay, Kevin. One last time. Open your mouth as wide as you can." Kevin did. Dr. Taylor sat down on the stool opposite Sam.

"First, his team did a technology assessment. They gave us a comprehensive analysis of all our technology along with detailed recommendations for fixing the issues they'd found. I was amazed.

They described many of the problems we were encountering on a regular basis. They seemed to have some kind of magical insight into our problems. The Guru called this 'wisdom.' Is that mouth open?"

Sam looked over at Kevin in time to see him snap his jaw open again. He looked like a snake preparing to devour a rhino.

"Anyway, we approved all their recommendations. They fixed everything, then trained us to use the EHR system. That's when we started to experience the productivity gains we had hoped for in the first place."

"Are you still using that system now?" Sam asked.

"No, we eventually moved to a new software system. And this time we had The EHR Guru work with us from the start. It was a very smooth process. That's what we're using today." He turned to look at Kevin. "Why are you sitting there with your mouth open?"

Kevin laughed. "You told me to!"

"Did I? I don't think so."

"You did!"

"Oh. Sorry. You can close it. I'm going to talk to your dad a little more. Is that okay?"

"I guess," Kevin said as he reached for his dinosaurs.

"What about maintenance?" Sam asked. "Or updates? Do you have people on staff to manage the technology for you?"

"No, that wouldn't be cost effective. I don't want to run an IT department. I leave all that to the Guru and his staff. We outsource all of our support to them. They're down in the city, but it's almost like they're part of our staff. Whenever the vendor has an update, or we install a new interface, I just send over the Guru's contact information. His team coordinates the details. I don't have to think twice.

"I tell you, Sam, I recommend them to everyone. That's who you need to be talking to."

"Thanks. I'll definitely be giving him a call."

"Good. I'll text him to emphasize you need help fast." He turned back to Kevin. "Well, Kevin, you've definitely got a cold, and maybe an infection in your throat. I'm going to send you to the pharmacy to get some antibiotics. You need to take your medicine, get plenty of rest, and drink lots of water. Okay?"

Kevin nodded, and Sam did, too.

"What pharmacy do you guys usually go to? I like the CVS here, but you're in Lakeville, aren't you?"

"Yes," Sam replied, "we usually go to Morgan's in Salisbury."

Dr. Taylor tapped on the computer. "There it is. Okay, no problem, I'll send it there. It's done!" He tapped some more. "I'm printing out some information about causes, symptoms, and prevention of throat problems for you to take with you. You can pick it up from Tara on your way out. We'll notify you of the test results from his throat culture tomorrow. Oh no, wait. That's Sunday. We'll get them on Monday.

"If you don't see changes in Kevin's condition in a few days, then give us a call. If he gets worse, call right away. Or just bring him in. Except not tomorrow."

"Thank you very much." Sam stood up and shook the doctor's hand. "For everything."

Chapter 6
The Pharmacy

Kevin was happily playing with his new toys as they drove out of the parking lot at Taylor Pediatrics. Sam kept hearing the sounds of an epic mini-dinosaur battle going on in the back seat and could not help but smile.

"You won't be eating any more dinosaurs today, Mr. Rex!" Kevin announced in his best triceratops voice. Sam figured he knew who had won the battle.

The bell on the door of Morgan's Pharmacy jingled as Sam shut it. His heels clicked on the old, wooden floor as he and Kevin walked down an aisle filled with gift soaps and children's toys. When they reached the counter at the rear of the store, they were greeted by one of the pharmacists, a tall, handsome man of about thirty.

"Hi, what can I do for you?"

"My name is Sam Bushman. We're here to pick up some antibiotics for my son, Kevin," he said, putting his hand on Kevin's shoulder.

"Ah yes, I saw that one from Dr. Taylor. Can I see your insurance card and driver's license?"

Sam was already reaching for his wallet.

"Thanks," said the pharmacist as he took the cards. He slid Kevin's insurance card through a scanner. Then he looked at the driver's license and then at Sam to confirm there was a match. "Well, Mr. Bushman, your son's prescription is almost ready." He pointed to a row of four chairs against the wall. "If you'd like to wait a few minutes." He handed back the cards.

"Great, thanks," Sam said. He looked around to make sure no one else was waiting. "Since we have a moment, could I ask you a couple questions about your computer system? For instance, how does it work? Why is it better than using paper prescriptions?"

The pharmacist looked surprised. Sam guessed most customers couldn't care less about the system the pharmacy used.

"Well, the thing I like most about our system is the fact I don't have to try to understand each doctor's handwriting. Before we got this system, we often had to contact the physician to confirm the prescriptions and dosage. Now we get everything printed out, not scribbles we have to second-guess."

"Anything else?" Sam prompted.

Again the pharmacist paused. "Are you a secret shopper or something?"

Sam laughed. "No. I'm the practice administrator for a group of orthopedists. We're thinking of getting an EHR system for our practice."

Once he realized he was talking to a fellow professional, the pharmacist became effusive. "Oh, you definitely should. I mean, I can't speak for your end, but on our end, it's great.

"For example, the system automatically updates data on the drugs we provide to our clients. All the information about the medications is ready to print for the patient—everything from side effects to allergy restrictions. It's really helpful. And it's much more efficient than doing everything manually, or trying to stock literature for every type of medication.

"But that's just why I like it. I've heard the biggest benefit of these things is the amount of errors they eliminate throughout the whole pharmacy system. Do you know how many people die each year because of medical errors?"

"Not really."

"Yeah, neither do I. But it's a lot. And—"

"Nearly two hundred thousand in the United States alone."

Sam and the pharmacist both turned to see who had spoken. Another pharmacist, shorter and balder than the first, was working at the adjacent counter.

The new guy looked up at his colleague. "It was in the booklet they gave us."

"And you memorized it?"

The shorter man ignored him and addressed Sam instead. "That number is for all deaths due to medical errors, including mistakes with medications. The booklet also described how these new systems in pharmacies are preventing a lot of patient deaths by reducing the number of mistakes."

"How do they do that?" Sam asked.

"The database makes sure we provide the correct medicine and dose. It also cross-references patient health records with drug databases to identify possible interactions with current medications. And it checks for adverse reactions to the new medicine based on patient history."

Sam checked on Kevin, who was refereeing Dino Smackdown 2 on one of the chairs. "What about transparency?"

"Everything that happens is documented. It can be viewed by the patient, the doctor who ordered the prescription, or anyone who assists with the patient's care."

"Well, you two sure seem to like it."

The first pharmacist clearly did not like being left out of the conversation. "It was like moving from black-and-white television to color," he said quickly.

Sam was impressed, but felt he'd heard enough. He turned the conversation back to his own case. "So what do I do if I need to refill my son's prescription?"

Again, the taller man jumped in. "You can order it through the patient portal of Dr. Taylor's system or through our store website. You can choose to pick it up here, or have it mailed to you. It's really easy," he said with a grin. "If you forget or lose your prescription, you can just sign on and find it quickly. Some patients also use other sites, like Google Health or Microsoft HealthVault, to track their prescriptions, and other health information, too."

A thought occurred to Sam. "Do all pharmacies have this capability now?"

The man clearly did not know. He seemed a bit dejected as he deferred to the other pharmacist.

"I saw a report that said as of March 2010, about five thousand U.S. pharmacies had EHR equivalents installed. We're the early adopters, but the rest will follow. As more and more medical offices get EHRs, pharmacies will have to get their own equivalent systems just to keep up."

Sam furrowed his brow. "So what you have isn't an EHR?"

"The shorter pharmacist shook his head. "No, those are just for doctor's offices. But our system connects with doctors' EHRs through an HIE." He glanced up at his colleague and grinned. Sam was sure he saw something evil in that grin. Then he looked back at Sam. "Here's something you should know. Do you remember the American Recovery and Reinvestment Act?"

"The stimulus bill?" Sam asked tentatively.

"That's right. It sets out new health information technology requirements. But it also provides funding for doctors who implement EHR systems in their medical practices."

The taller man seemed annoyed. "What are you, an encyclopedia?"

Sam ignored him. "That's good for me. Does it cover you guys, too?"

"No, the government money's just for EHRs." A phone rang, and the taller pharmacist went to answer it. His colleague continued, "But either way, we have to keep up with all the advances in the medical field if we want to stay in business."

A pharmacy tech placed a paper bag on the counter, "Here's your son's prescription. Your copay is twenty dollars." Sam took a card out of his wallet and swiped it through the reader. He touched the screen in the appropriate places, then signed the slip and the prescription pick-up log.

The second pharmacist was still nearby. "Do you mind if I ask why you're so interested in our technology?"

"I'm the practice administrator for a medical group. I need to figure out how to install an EHR system for our practice."

"Oh," the pharmacist smiled. "No wonder. Y'know, you'll need an expert to help you make a smooth transition from your current paper-based system." He opened a drawer and rummaged through it. "It's a big change. A positive one, but a big one. I have a card here somewhere from an IT group many of the local physicians use. Here it is."

"Great, thanks." Sam knew what would be on the card before he even took it. As he headed out the door with Kevin, he wondered why everyone in town seemed to know about The EHR Guru but him.

As soon as they got home, Sam turned both Kevin and the medicine over to Alina. While Alina put the medicine into Kevin and Kevin into his bed with his portable DVD player, Sam retired to the master bedroom. It was there, in a large but not particularly comfortable upholstered armchair, that Sam sometimes went to think. On this occasion, though, he didn't think so much as imagine.

Sam imagined what a new patient would see when arriving at MedOne for the first time. After visiting Taylor Pediatrics, he realized that his own office seemed low-tech and … dilapidated. He marveled that his receptionists could get any work done with the mess of papers around the front desk. Patients were not usually greeted with a smile or a Tyrannosaurus Rex. Granted, most of their orthopedic patients probably wouldn't want a little dinosaur toy, but perhaps there was something else they would like. Sam made a note to think about that later.

As he continued his mental tour of the practice, he saw doctors holding clipboards and ball-point pens, writing exam notes and prescriptions by hand, and conversing about patient history. The clipboards were far from efficient and definitely not as attractive as the shiny tablet computers Dr. Taylor used.

Sam took a deep breath, got out the card the pharmacist had given him, and dialed the number of The EHR Guru. His heartbeat kicked up its pace a little. He exhaled slowly as the phone rang. A woman's voice greeted him.

"Hello, The EHR Guru. This is Sophia. How may I direct your call?"

That caught Sam by surprise. He'd thought the EHR Guru was just one guy. "Umm … yeah. Hi, my name is Sam Bushman. I was just calling for the EHR Guru."

"Okay, can I tell him what the call is about?"

"I'm the administrator at a medical practice. Dr. Kurt Taylor referred me to him."

"Did you get a T-Rex?" Clearly, Sophia was familiar with Dr. Taylor's office.

Sam laughed. "No, but my son did. He actually got two—a T-Rex and a triceratops," Sam replied, feeling more comfortable.

"Good! Maybe he'll share with you. One moment, please." Sophia put him on hold. It only took about ten seconds before the renowned Guru picked up the line.

"Sam! How's it going? Dr. Taylor texted that you'd be calling. What can I do for you?"

"Well, I work for Dr. Karen Metz at MedOne Orthopedics in Sharon, Connecticut. The majority of our systems are paper-based, and it's killing us. I have been told to find a solution." Or find another job, Sam thought to himself.

The Guru chuckled. "Sam, I know this is all a bit overwhelming. I've heard that tone you have in your voice more times than I can count. It may seem like you're in big trouble, but I have good news for you: EHR systems work. This will help you improve productivity and profitability and make your organization an almost paperless practice."

"Wow. I gotta tell you, those sound like some rather lofty claims."

"They are, and I stand by them, Sam. Electronic record-keeping systems are sweeping the healthcare industry and becoming vital to the very infrastructure of it. Even the government has realized this."

"Yeah, I know. I can get money to help pay for the changeover."

"You've done your homework. But it's more than that. If you don't get on board, the government may eventually even penalize you with lower reimbursements."

"Oh. Really? How do you know that?"

"I know this, Sam, because The EHR Guru has been getting dozens of requests from practices to help them evaluate, select, and implement EHR systems."

At first, it sounded to Sam as if the man was referring to himself in the third person. Then he remembered "The EHR Guru" was the name of the company as well as the guy's nickname.

"Can you tell me something about your company?"

"I started this business twenty-five years ago from a spare bedroom in my house. Now, thanks to an increasingly IT-dependent world, I have a team of talented employees. We mostly serve the New York metro tri-state area, but we have clients throughout the country. My people are the best, Sam. I know that "the Guru" has become my nickname, but actually I consider everyone on my team to be a guru.

"And Sam, over the ten years of doing EHR implementations, we've actually had a one-hundred-percent success rate."

Although he'd been leaning that way all morning, it was then that Sam finally made his decision. "It sounds like I have a lot to learn in the two weeks that Karen will be gone. How do I get started?"

"Two weeks? In that case, we need to meet sooner rather than later. Can you be at our offices in Long Island City at eight o'clock Monday morning?"

"Sure! That would be great."

Chapter 7

The EHR Guru

After the excitement wore off, Sam realized that it would not be easy driving from Lakeville to Long Island City in rush-hour traffic. Google Maps told him the drive would take 2 hours and 4 minutes, but he knew better. Sunday night, he set his alarm for five o'clock. Monday morning he showered, dressed, and sat down at the kitchen table to have breakfast and prepare for the meeting. By the time his cereal bowl was empty, he had filled three pages of his notepad with questions.

During the drive, he could not help wondering what he was going to do if all his efforts failed. He couldn't imagine getting another job as a practice administrator—they don't open up that often, and someone who'd just been fired from that position would not make an ideal candidate. Could he get a job as an assistant administrator somewhere? Could he and Alina make do on the reduced salary? Could he move back to Seattle and run his dad's practice?

As he parked on the street in front of The EHR Guru's office, he resolved to do his best, regardless of the outcome.

The street was lined with trees, and the Guru's building was built of light-colored stone. It was six stories tall, but seemed long and low because it took up the whole block. Sam went in the door and took the elevator to the sixth floor.

Sophia greeted him with a smile and directed him down a hallway to a conference room. As Sam reached for the door handle, the image of the short, bearded, Indian man popped into his head again.

"Sam! Come on in and take a seat." The Guru turned out to be tall, white, and clean-shaven. The room was comfortable, with a wide, polished-wood table surrounded by rolling office chairs. Sam was surprised to see that the walls were covered with whiteboards, but then realized he should have expected it.

As they shook hands and then both sat down, Sam sized up the man across from him. The Guru's nonchalant grin belied a zeal in his eyes Sam hadn't expected. It was obvious this guy was a confident businessman.

"So, I'm sure you have a lot of questions for me, Sam. But before you start, let me ask you a few questions and then give you some information. Perhaps I might answer a few of your questions in the process."

"Fire away."

The questions the Guru asked about Sam and his practice were very thorough, ranging from the number of practitioners, exam rooms, and patient visits per month to the types of procedures they performed, what labs they used, and what types of diagnostic instruments they owned. It was nearly half an hour before the Guru set his iPad aside.

"Let me explain a few things about EHR technology, Sam. That will help you understand what to expect when working with our company and while using an EHR system.

"First of all, each medical practice is unique. Depending on the focus of the practice, the design of the EHR system will vary. For instance, the needs of an orthopedic practice with eight exam rooms and five practitioners at one location are different than an OB/GYN practice with twenty exam rooms, fifteen practitioners, and three locations."

"Well, yeah. That makes sense."

"Point two: To fully implement a comprehensive EHR solution, you will almost surely work with technology and software from more than one vendor.   And the complexity increases if the system must be accessible in real time at multiple locations."

"We only have the one location."

"Yes, but you might want to be integrated with, say, hospitals, labs, diagnostic devices, a patient recall system, a billing clearinghouse, an insurance-eligibility checking service .... The vendors we'll be dealing with try to design their software and equipment with interconnectivity in mind.   Nonetheless, to connect everything together in a way that creates a seamless system takes time, creativity, and yes, maybe even a little wisdom."

Sam grinned.   "Dr. Taylor said you provide that."

"He's right.   We do."

At first, Sam had assumed that the Guru's confidence came from a salesman-type personality.   He was beginning to realize, though, something else was going on.   The Guru had done this many times before, and had a clear vision of both the process and the outcome.

"In most EMR implementations, patient service is dependent on system uptime."

"Uptime to where?" Sam interjected.   "I'm a little weak on my tech terms."

The Guru smiled.   "Uptime means the time the system is up and running.   What happens to a medical practice if the power goes out?   Well, if they're working with paper charts, they can open the window blinds and continue seeing patients.   But once the EHR system is in place, any downtime will affect patient service and practically shut down the practice.   Thus the uptime of the technology is paramount to success."   He wrote some numbers on his yellow pad.   "It's a point we pride ourselves on at The EHR

Guru—that and being able to handle the complexity of most EHR systems."

He slid the pad across the table to Sam. It read "99.615%."

"That is the average uptime we've achieved over the last three years. In other words, the hardware we install and support has been continuously in service during office hours, without crashing, almost one hundred percent of the time over the last three years. That's the main benefit you receive when you outsource your IT support to The EHR Guru."

"I can see that. But how do you manage it?"

"We keep our people certified in the latest technologies, and we regularly review new EHR systems. We're constantly learning and constantly improving our internal processes while expanding our wisdom to support a wide array of technology. This allows us to troubleshoot unexpected problems faster than any in-house IT department."

"I'm sorry, what in-house IT departments are you referring to?"

"The one you would set up if you wanted to support your EHR system yourself."

"Oh! Yeah, no. That's ... that's not really an option for me. Us."

The Guru smiled warmly. "That's fine. Our goal is to take care of your technology so your doctors can take care of your patients."

Sam was surprised at how flustered he'd gotten. Clearly he wasn't as comfortable with all this tech stuff as he'd thought he was. He concentrated harder as the Guru continued.

"With an EHR system, data security is very important. In fact, security and privacy are two of the key tenets of Meaningful Use."

"Oh! I know that one!" Sam interrupted. "If we can show we have Meaningful Use of the system, the government will help us pay for it."

"That's right. And all the systems we install are certified and comply with the security and privacy mandates for Meaningful Use.

"We also implement a backup system—called a Total Server Protection service or 'TSP'—which backs up all your data both at your office and off-site. If your system goes down, you can have your entire EMR up and running again off of one of our TSP systems in about a half-hour. Or, in the event of a catastrophe such as a fire, we can provision a new TSP unit almost overnight, so you can at least have access to your patient records. We test these systems monthly to ensure they will work as planned in the event they are needed. We do everything we can to protect your business.

"Once the system is in place and your staff is trained to use it, your practice will benefit from a vastly improved office workflow. Billing, scheduling, prescription writing, patient-visit notes, histories, and allergies will all be accessible via the EHR system. If you want, you can set up remote access for designated staff members to connect to the EMR system from anywhere with an internet connection. So if, for example, a physician needs to review some X-rays at home the night before an operation, they can do that from their home computer using their personal login.

"Your patients will also benefit from an online location where they can interact with your system. I assume you've already experienced Taylor Pediatrics' patient portal?"

I used it, Sam thought. I don't know if I've "experienced" it. Out loud, he said, "Yes."

"That's just one type, of course. Depending on your choice of software, MedOne's patient portal might look and function differently.

"Finally, your EHR software doesn't have to be the only program running on your new system. You can leverage this investment in technology to improve the workflow in other, non-clinical areas of the practice. We have clients who use their systems to improve office communications via the use of email. Then you could have an e-mail address like 'S Bushman at Med One Ortho dot com,' or whatever your domain name is. Others have asked us to set up fax servers, or to place their accounting programs on the new system. Do you guys have a website?"

Sam was hesitant to answer. The MedOne website was not something to be proud of. "Yes we do, but it's very simple...and we could use a MedOne email system."

"Okay, no problem. The quality of the EHR system is what's important here. All your website has to do is direct your patients to the portal." The Guru took a deep breath and thought for a moment. "I've covered quite a bit and given you a rather comprehensive introduction. Did I answer some of your questions?"

"Yes, you did, as a matter of fact. It's going to take me a while to digest all that you've said. There are a couple things I still need to know, though: timing and cost of implementation."

"Well, implementation timeframes range from three months to a year. However, with practices your size, we usually shoot for—and hit—a six-month target for complete integration. This includes setup and staff training.

"As far as price, we need to do a technology assessment to evaluate your current technology. You'll need a high-performance, stable, supportable backbone on which to host your EMR system. Based on the assessment, we might recommend upgrades to achieve that, or suggest you connect to a system hosted outside your office. Those upgrades are a big component of the cost.

"The final cost will also depend on the EHR system you choose. We often recommend several possible programs and leave the final decision to you. Choosing the right EHR software is really important because everyone in your office is affected by its structure and design. If it's too complex for your practice or difficult to navigate, your efficiency suffers and your patience is tested."

At first Sam heard that as, "Your patients is tested." While it was grammatically incorrect, he realized, it was probably true. With the wrong system, both their patience and their patients would be tested.

"Also, the software needs to be certified to qualify your practice for Meaningful Use. If you qualify, obviously, that will bring the cost way down. During our technology assessment, we may pinpoint other areas of the practice that would also benefit from this investment in new technology. If you choose to add email or accounting or other options, that obviously increases the total cost. The costs of all the options will be included in the report we submit after the technology assessment."

He finally paused, allowing Sam to squeeze more questions in.

"Is the assessment free? And how long does it take?"

"Ah yes, you have a deadline." The Guru leaned back in his chair.

"Ideally, I should have a plan in-hand by the time my boss returns."

"You said two weeks? That's not a lot of time, but we can do it. And yes, there is a fee for the technology assessment. But if you contract right away and allow my team to visit MedOne's offices over the next few days, we can have you ready for your boss when she gets back. We could start in two business days and be back to you with a completed assessment one week later."

Sam smiled. "Show me the contract."

The Guru flipped through a stack of papers in front of him. "While my team looks over your practice, I'm going to send you to a friend of mine to get a better look at the operational side of an EHR system."

He passed a contract across to Sam. Sitting on top of it was a business card. "He's a cardiologist who's also a client. I think you'll find his practice is similar to MedOne, except they have an EHR system installed and supported by my team. You'll be able to get a very clear picture of how an EHR system works from the perspective of the doctors and nurses at his practice."

"I guess I have a steep learning curve ahead of me."

"Yes, you do," the Guru confirmed. "When you give your presentation for your boss in two weeks, you'll want to show off your extensive knowledge. But we're going to get you up to speed on all aspects of an EHR system as quickly as we can." He stood up, signaling that the meeting was over. "Before you visit Dr. Daniels, could you just call your office and make sure they know my people will be stopping by to start the assessment? Don't worry, they'll call to schedule the visit in advance."

Sam was checking the business card in front of him. Ben Daniels was the Guru's cardiologist client. "Huh? Oh, sure. I can do that."

The Guru slapped a large hand on Sam's back. "No worries Sam! It's time for you to get schooled in EHR!"

Chapter 8
The Cardiologist

As soon as he reached his car, Sam pulled out his new cell phone and called Dr. Daniels's office. The receptionist seemed to be expecting his call and gave him a one-o'clock appointment.

The office was in Westchester County, which meant it was basically on Sam's way home. After checking his map a few times, and getting lost a few times, Sam cruised past the cardiology practice just before twelve-thirty. This gave him time to grab a quick lunch. The sandwich shop he chose at random turned out to have his favorite: Philly cheese steak. As he wolfed it down, Sam thought about the good luck he'd had since leaving the Guru's office. Was it an omen?

On the way up to Dr. Daniels's office, Sam shared the elevator with an older, white-haired man. When they both got off at the same floor, then both reached for the same office door, Sam found out that the man was Dr. Daniels himself.

He's got to be at least sixty-five, Sam thought. If he can learn to use all this technology, I should be able to, too. He knew he was just feeding into a stereotype. But it made him feel better, so he held onto it.

Dr. Daniels led Sam back to his office. As they walked down the hall, the cardiologist boasted about his ability to view test results and X-rays from his summer house in the Hamptons and access the system from his iPhone. Inside the office, he closed the door, waved Sam to a chair, and sat down behind his desk.

"Well," he said, "I'm happy to help the Guru however I can. Unfortunately, I don't have a lot of time. What do you need from me?"

"I'd like to understand how your system works. I mean, what it's like to use it. So I can explain to the doctors in my practice what they can expect."

Dr. Daniels stood back up. "Well, the best thing to do, then, is for you to sit right here."

Sam moved to the chair behind the desk. Dr. Daniels reached past Sam to tap a few keys on his keyboard. The computer woke up, and the monitor was filled with boxes, labels, and links. It was pleasingly organized, and not at all cluttered.

"This is my 'physician's dashboard.' Each doctor here has one, and we can customize them to a certain extent. It's like a ... central information hub. When I log into the system, I'm automatically taken here. It's like my launch pad to the rest of the system."

Standing behind Sam, Dr. Daniels pointed out where on the dashboard he could find his daily schedule, urgent messages, reminders, new lab results, and items requiring his signature or approval. He also showed Sam how the system automatically reminds him to check in with certain patients throughout the year.

"Now, I can't show you a patient's record, of course. But you should see what they look like. So I'm going to show you mine, if that's alright with you."

"You're your own patient?"

"Well, not my patient, no. I see one of the other doctors in the practice. I've got no choice. I made sure all the best cardiologists around work right here!"

"Okay, sure. I mean, if you're okay with it. I don't want to intrude."

"Ahh, I don't think I've got anything much to hide."

For the first time, Sam looked at the system as though he were a doctor. Dr. Daniels showed him how to call up his records, and then how to click through them so he could see first-hand the documentation on the patient's health, vital signs, and lab results. (He was impressed to learn that Dr. Daniels was seventy-two years old.) He could see how all of the consultation notes from each visit were available to view, sorted chronologically. An alert popped up, indicating Dr. Daniels needed to reorder medication. With the doctor's guidance, Sam transmitted the prescription electronically.

"That was simple," Sam said. But he was impressed with himself nonetheless.

They continued navigating through the system. At one point, Dr. Daniels mentioned they encouraged new patients to bring with them a CD-ROM or USB drive containing any previous X-rays. They could upload the images into the system, and the doctor would always have access to them.

"I'm glad I'm not a patient of yours," Sam said. "I'd have no idea how to get my X-rays onto a CD."

"Ah, but your radiologist knows how." Dr. Daniels turned to face Sam. "Before the Guru installed our EHR system, we used to have an employee lounge in the back. I thought it would be a great idea to display the charts of patients who were currently experiencing serious issues. That way, when people get to work, they're reminded of who we're helping and why our patients need us.

"Well, it started off as a good idea, but pretty soon the room became a place nobody ever wanted to visit. It became so cluttered with charts, diagrams, and X-rays—it was a huge mess. It became more of a storeroom than an employee lounge."

He turned around to face the desk and began clicking the mouse. "Now look at this." He pointed to the screen. "We moved all that information into the system. Then the room became an employee lounge again. Everybody loves it. We were also able to empty an adjacent room full of files and create a Stress Buster suite for our patients. It's a triple win." He counted on his fingers as he spoke. "The staff gets a place to relax and eat lunch, the patients have a brand-new treatment option, and the practice gets a source of additional revenue."

Sam knew Karen would love to have a new source of revenue for MedOne, but he doubted that their orthopedics patients needed a Stress Buster suite, whatever that was. He decided that those kinds of changes were a distraction from his primary mission. "I've been to one practice already where they use tablet computers a lot. I don't see any tablets around here. Do you think they're useful?"

"Sure, tablet computers can very useful. However, we've found that simply having a workstation in each room meets our needs. Besides, if you drop a tablet and break the screen, then the whole computer becomes useless. We don't carry workstations, so they don't get dropped."

Sam was about to ask another question, but he saw that Dr. Daniels was looking at his watch. Sam knew there was a clock in the bottom right corner of the computer monitor. The fact that the doctor had checked his watch and not the computer made Sam like him a little bit more.

"Well, I'm afraid my time is up," the doctor said. "Why don't I show you one of the workstations? You can spend a few minutes kicking the tires." He picked up the phone and asked if there was an exam room that would be empty for a while.

As he led Sam down the corridor, Dr. Daniels explained that every workstation contained a computer, which for some reason he called a "thin client computer." All the client computers were connected to something called a "terminal server host." Sam gathered that the host was the brains of the operation, and the "thin" computers were pretty much just access points. Dr. Daniels went on to explain the security and utility of the terminal server.

They passed an open doorway. Inside, Sam noticed a couch and a massage chair, and he assumed he was looking at the employee lounge. Recent issues of Popular Science and Golf sat on the coffee table. A refrigerator hummed, and the door clicked as one of the nurses looked inside for an afternoon snack.

When they got to the exam room, Dr. Daniels pointed out the workstation. Sam was pretty sure he could have found it on his own. It looked like an ordinary desktop monitor and keyboard. The monitor was thin, but not unusually so. He wondered why it was called a thin computer.

"Is there anything I can get you?" Dr. Daniels asked.

Sam thought a moment. He wondered about the wider implications of the EHR dashboard and so on. He was starting to understand how it helped the doctors, but needed to learn more about its impact on the rest of the staff.

"Could I possibly talk to some of the other staff members here? I'd like to get a better view of the system from, say, a nurse's perspective."

"I thought you might say that. I know just the right person."

Chapter 9
Nurse Gabe

Dr. Daniels reappeared a minute later. With him was a short, stocky man in scrubs. "Gabe," Dr. Daniels said, "this is Sam Bushman. Gabe was our chief liaison to the Guru and his staff while they were installing our EHR system. They called him a 'super user.'"

Sam stood and shook Gabe's hand. The nurse had olive skin and a mustache that made Sam jealous.

"Dr. Daniels said you want to learn about our EHR system from a nurse's perspective?"

"Yeah, I'm trying to get an EHR system at our orthopedic practice. I need to be able to tell the staff what it will do for them. If you don't mind."

"Do you mind if I eat while we talk?"

He held up a brown paper bag, and Sam realized that Gabe had been getting his lunch, not a snack, from the refrigerator when they'd walked past. "No, of course not."

"Then I'm happy to help."

Gabe drew a second chair up to the workstation. Sam looked around for Dr. Daniels to thank him again, but the man had already left.

"So, Sam, what have you seen already?" Gabe asked.

Sam sat down in front of the monitor. "I've seen the physician's dashboard and how a doctor can manage all of her activities in the system. I'd like to see what an EHR system is going to look like for our nurses. It'd be great if you could walk me through your daily activities. You know, show me how you interact with the system and how it benefits you."

"Fair enough," Gabe said. "But our job doesn't start here. It starts out front."

"At the reception desk?"

"Yes. You know how it works up to that point? The patient schedules an appointment, the receptionist logs the patient in, and the patient waits in the waiting area."

"Yeah, I just did that recently with an appointment for my son."

Gabe looked concerned. "Here?"

"No, at his pediatrician's."

"That's good. I hate it when kids have to see a cardiologist. It's not right. Anyway, a nurse will bring the patient from the waiting room to the exam room. But before that, it is our responsibility to review the EHR system for the chief complaint, their medical history, their health background, and any personal notes on them. That will help us to personalize our conversation."

He paused a minute to think. "You want to know how the EHR system affects a nurse's interaction with a patient? First, imagine a patient's visit as a series of interactions between the patient and the different people here. The start and end of these interactions are called 'experience bookends.' Hopefully, the patient experienced a positive initial experience bookend at the reception desk. Our job as nurses is to build upon that as we transition the patient to the doctor."

"'Initial experience bookend.' Why don't you just call it the first interaction?"

Gabe smiled broadly. "I don't know, brother. The boss made up the terms, not me."

Sam grinned, too. "Okay, let me ask you this: Why do you focus more on the beginning and end of the patient's visit? Isn't their time with the doctor what's most important? From the patient's point of view, I mean."

"First of all, everyone in our medical practice is responsible for providing a positive patient experience. Everyone shares a responsibility to anticipate and respond to patient needs and desires promptly, professionally, and pleasantly."

"No offense, but that sounded kind of like a canned speech."

Gabe smiled again. "Just because it's memorized doesn't mean it isn't true. It's something we take very seriously here."

"I can see that." Sam glanced over at the paper bag. "You should start eating. I don't want to take away your lunch hour."

Gabe pulled out a Tupperware container, a fork, and a napkin. He opened the container and dug into the salad inside it. After chewing a bit, he continued.

"Where was I? Oh, yes. Mistakes and delays and problems can happen any time, from when the patient walks in the door to when he walks out at the end. But it turns out that what we remember most is the first thing that happens and the last thing that happens. That's why we focus on the experience bookends."

"But it's more than that," Gabe continued. "How we start and finish each individual patient interaction is critical, too. Our EHR system helps us transition the patient through each stage of the visit and overcome unexpected challenges."

"Such as?"

Gabe thought a moment. "Okay. Last week, one of our more elderly patients arrived without an appointment. He plopped a bottle of pills down in front of the receptionist and told her he had run out of meds and needed a new prescription.

"Now, the receptionists can schedule appointments, but the EHR system does not allow them to view any confidential medical information. So she politely asked the man to wait while she checked with his doctor. The doctor was with another patient, so she asked me to help."

"You were free?"

"No, but I made myself free. I checked the patient's health records in the system, and the receptionist checked the system to see if Dr. Fisher had an opening in her schedule. I found out that the patient was about to finish his current prescription and was scheduled for a consult with Dr. Fisher the following week. The receptionist found out that Dr. Fisher had an opening after his next appointment. She fit the man into it and sent the doctor a notification that his open slot had been filled.

"So Dr. Fisher missed a little break, and our elderly patient was a little angry about having to wait twenty minutes. But he got a new prescription that day and left quite satisfied. Without the EHR system, it would have taken much longer than it did to coordinate all those activities."

Sam pictured how the same event would have played out at MedOne. "Instead of your receptionist being defensive, denying help, making the client wait for a long time in your reception area, or the situation escalating in some other negative way. "

"Exactly."

"It's interesting that your receptionist had the authority to book that appointment on such short notice for Dr. Fisher. Isn't that exasperating for the doctor when he's mentally prepared to take a break?"

Gabe said, "No," and to Sam it sounded, not like "No, he didn't," but rather, "No, you've got it wrong."

"Remember," he continued, "everyone in our organization is committed to providing a superior patient experience on every visit, every phone call, and every client interaction. Including our doctors. The EHR enables all our employees to take more responsibility for that positive customer experience. It lets us make more decisions on our own."

"Impressive."

"Anyway, you wanted to see what the system looks like for the nurses?"

"Yes, please."

Gabe pulled the keyboard into his lap and started typing. Sam realized that while the workstation had a monitor and a keyboard, there was no computer. Instead, the two devices were wired into a box about the size of a hardcover book. Maybe that's the "thin client," he thought.

"When I log in," Gabe said, "I immediately see this Patient Manager home screen. See these icons on the left?" A number of tiles ran down the left side of the screen. Each one contained an icon of a person with a name underneath it. "This is the Practice tab. These are the patients I served this morning," he said, pointing, "and these are the ones coming in later today. This is the part of the system I interact with the most, because it's where we enter vitals, document visits, et cetera.

"See these other sections?" He pointed at the words that ran along the top of the screen: Admin, Recalls, Referrals, Messages, Documents, and Billing. "These sections are where all the other stuff happens." His finger stopped on Messages. "When the receptionist sent that notification to Dr. Fisher about his break time being booked? I also logged onto the system and sent him a note about the situation."

"Sounds like a lot of email."

"It's better than not knowing what's going on and having to ask the patient all over again. Patients hate that."

Sam smiled ruefully. "Yes, I know."

"Oh! Check this out. This is really cool!" Gabe started clicking the mouse, navigating quickly through the system. "About a month ago, we had a female patient who had been experiencing cardiovascular issues—pain in her chest, tingling in her fingers, stuff like that. She called on the phone and asked to talk to a nurse. The only nurse available was a first-year without a lot of experience. But once she updated the patient's records with the new complaints, the system prompted her with what questions to ask."

"You're kidding."

"Check it out, brother." He clicked the cursor into a box labeled Chief Complaints, and handed the keyboard to Sam.

Sam typed in *chest pain*. Immediately, a list headed *Further Questions* popped up:

- Has the patient had any blunt trauma to the chest?

- Does the patient smoke?

- Does the patient have a family history of heart disease?

- Is the patient experiencing an uncomfortable pressure, fullness, squeezing or pain in the center of the chest lasting more than a few minutes?

- Does the patient take any medication for a chronic heart condition?

"We usually know all these first-level questions, but when you go deeper, it can be very helpful. Go ahead, ask me."

Sam played the part of the nurse, asking patient Gabe each of the questions. Gabe showed him how to input the patient's answers, and how each response led to a new series of questions.

"I am seriously impressed," Sam said.

"Right? And it's not just for phone calls. When we set up a patient profile, the system prompts us with questions, too. For me, this is the most important function of the system. Each patient is assigned to a specific doctor. But we nurses, we have to serve everyone, at any time. We deal with hundreds of patients a week. And having this information available can be absolutely crucial."

"I can see that."

Gabe took an apple out of the bag and put the fork and empty container in. For the rest of his lunch hour, he led Sam step by step through the EHR system. First he let Sam set up a fictitious patient profile. Then they walked through what a nurse does to prepare for a patient's visit, and how he completes the beginning of the exam by entering the patient's vitals in the system. Before long, Sam was convinced, not only that the system would help MedOne deliver a better patient experience, but that the nurses there would love it.

When they were done, Sam felt comfortable enough with the system to tackle a task on his own. He clicked on the *Messages* tab and sent a note to Dr. Daniels:

Subject: Thanks from Sam

Hi Dr. Daniels,

This is great. Thanks for letting me have a look around! Gabe has been very helpful. Give him a raise.

Sam

Chapter 10
The Focus Group

Without traffic or bad weather, Dr. Daniels's office was an hour and a half away from MedOne. As Sam drove through the pouring rain, he got hung up at two different accidents before he reached the office. By the time he'd dealt with the most pressing of his day-to-day tasks and driven home, it was well after nine o'clock, and he was exhausted. After wiping his shoes and hanging up his soaking overcoat, he locked the door and went to check on everyone. Kevin was fast asleep in his room, clutching his now-familiar T-Rex. Alina looked up as he opened their bedroom door. She was already under the covers, reading a book.

"So, how'd the interview go? Did they confess?"

Sam slumped against the doorframe and smiled. "They gave away all their secrets."

"And the buried treasure? Did they finally give up the location?"

"Not quite, but I did find some more clues." He came and sat on the bed. "I'm going to grab a bite and do a quick email check. How was Kevin today?"

"Fine, no complaints at all when he got home." She suddenly sat up straight and placed her finger lightly on his lips. "Shhh! Can you hear that?"

Sam strained his ears. "I don't hear anything."

"Exactly! No coughs or wheezes. He's sleeping like a log." She leaned back into her pillow. "Now go feed your face and check your emails."

Peeking in at Kevin again on his way past, Sam wondered where the triceratops was—until he accidentally kicked it at the top of the stairs and sent it flying down to the landing. After making himself a peanut butter and jelly sandwich dinner, he carried it into the den and fired up the computer. He hadn't bothered to check his email in the office because he so rarely used email for work purposes. He took a bite of the sandwich and waited for his computer to boot up.

Sam shifted the sandwich to his other hand and clicked on the AOL icon. Once he heard the familiar "You've got mail!" he clicked on the button with that sentence on it. His heart gave a little lurch when he saw the first message was from DrKurtTaylor. Was something wrong with Kevin's test results? Then he read the subject line and relaxed. He clicked to open the message.

From: DrKurtTaylor@taylorpediatrics.com
To: sbushman1974@aol.com
Subject: "EHR Patient Focus Group on Friday -- Are You Interested?"

Hello Sam,

After we talked last week, I forgot to mention that Taylor Pediatrics conducts regular focus groups of our patients. Our next meeting is this Friday. It is a rather informal affair, but it might be a great way for you to receive feedback about our EHR system's effectiveness from the patient's perspective. The meeting starts at around 2pm here at our main offices in town if you are interested. Just talk to Tara when you arrive, and she will direct you to the right room.

Take care!

Sincerely,

Kurt Taylor, MD
Taylor Pediatrics Group P.C.
DrKurtTaylor@taylorpediatrics.com
(860) 555-7376

Sam realized that for all the time and effort he'd spent researching EHRs, he had yet to hear from or speak to any patients at a practice that had an EHR system. This focus group could provide some valuable information. He would find out on Friday.

When Sam walked back through the doors of Taylor Pediatrics, he was pleased to see Tara and her pet dinosaur keeping guard over the waiting room. She directed him to the room where the focus group was being held.

The door had a small window in it. Sam peeked through and saw a group of what looked like parents and their kids sitting around a large table. All the adults and several of the children were looking at the head of the table. There, an older man in a white lab coat with long, silver hair pulled back into a ponytail was speaking. Sam opened the door.

"—to find out what you like and don't like about our system," the man was saying. "And this must be him now."

Sam didn't know whether to address the man or the entire group. He ended up doing something in between. "Hi. I'm Sam Bushman."

The man in the lab coat got up to shake Sam's hand. "It's great to have you here, Sam. I'm one of the doctors with the group. My name is Dr. Dennis Vitale."

It always annoyed Sam when doctors did that. His name was Dennis Vitale. "Doctor" was not part of his name. After all, Sam didn't come in and say, "My name is Mr. Sam Bushman." But he knew it was a small point, and besides, it seemed to him as if all doctors did it.

"I'm the facilitator for our group today," Dr. Vitale continued. "I've explained why you're here, and everyone has agreed to share their experiences with you." To the group he said,

"Sam is also a parent here, like you. He brought his son in for a visit last week."

"Cool," exclaimed one excited young boy with a slight build who looked to be about nine years old.

"Thanks for your feedback, Jerry." Dr. Vitale motioned for Sam to take an empty seat. "Jerry here broke his tibia last summer, didn't you, sir?"

"Yep!" Jerry said proudly. As confirmation, he lifted up his pants leg to show off the scar running up his shin. "Jumped a whole flight of stairs with a wheelbarrow! ...Kinda."

"Do you think Mr. Bushman should install a new computer system in his office?" Dr. Vitale asked.

"Sure!"

"And why is that?"

"Because of the whooshing sound," replied Jerry decisively.

"The whooshing sound?" Sam didn't get it.

"I can answer that one," replied the young woman sitting next to Jerry. "Hi, I'm Tina, the mom. The program makes a whooshing sound when we renew a prescription online. Most of the time I do it from the computer in the kitchen while he's eating breakfast. So he got used to hearing the sound." The adults chuckled.

"I'll have to check that sound out, Jerry," Sam said. "Thanks."

"No problem."

Sam looked around at the adults. "Does anyone use the system for something other than making appointments or refilling prescriptions?"

A middle-aged woman sitting next to a quiet girl of about twelve raised her hand. Dr. Vitale nodded at the woman. She put her hand down and cleared her throat. "Hello, my name's Donna. This is my daughter, Alia." She put her hand on the girl's hand. "Can you say hi, Alia?" Alia smiled, but leaned into her mom's side and hid her face.

Wrapping her arms around her daughter, Donna continued. "Alia's older brother Khalid is in med school right now. And as any good older brother should be, Khalid's a bit overprotective. So when Alia was diagnosed with the Coxsackie virus, he naturally wanted to know all about her test results and medications and things. I couldn't even understand some of his questions, never mind answering them. So I just told him how to get into the patient portal. He got all the information he needed there."

"I remember Khalid," Dr. Vitale said. "He sent me an email that night with questions about her dosages. Your son has a very sharp mind."

Donna beamed. "Thank you." She turned back to Sam. "Then Alia's grandmother called, and was she in a state! I mean, it's some strange virus we'd never heard of before. And if there's one thing my mother-in-law is good at ..." She put her hands over Alia's ears, "... it's flying off the handle. When I couldn't explain about the Coxsackie virus enough to calm her down, I pointed her towards the portal as well. The next day she called back, only now she's giving me advice on what to do with Alia!"

As he listened to the patients discuss their experiences with the EHR system and their PHRs, Sam found it particularly amusing to get the children's reactions to different functions of the system. For example, one little guy named Neil thought it was funny whenever the automated appointment reminder system phoned his house—or as he put it, "When the robot calls us." His mother explained how he insisted on pressing the buttons to confirm, reschedule, or cancel an appointment when prompted.

Then the only other dad in the room, a man named Chris, spoke up.

"All of this stuff is great. It's helpful, it's convenient .... But even if the system did none of that, it would still be invaluable because of what happened after the fire."

All of the parents nodded and "Mmmm"ed and clucked. Sam's confusion must have shown on his face, because Chris turned to address him directly.

"This office used to be around the corner, in the strip mall there. One day about nine months ago, I brought Nili in because she'd been having headaches and trouble sleeping for a few nights." Sam looked at the two girls next to him, both texting like mad, and wondered which one was Nili. "The doctor heard fluid in her lungs and thought it might be pneumonia. He drew some blood and sent it out for testing. He said it would take two days to get the results back.

"That night, the strip mall burns down. No one was hurt, thank God, but six businesses were completely destroyed." Chris straightened up in his chair. "At this point, my only concern was for Nili. What's going to happen to her tests and charts now that they've turned to ashes? How are they going to make her better when all of the computers that recorded her visit were melted down to puddles?

"I really had no idea what to do. I called the regular number when I was supposed to—I figured I'd get a recording or something. But someone answered the phone. She told me that the test was positive, and she made an appointment for Nili to come in again. It wasn't until she gave me an address in Winsted that I realized I'd been talking to a satellite office."

Dr. Vitale filled in some of the background. "The IT folks who support Taylor Pediatrics manage some type of online backup system. When they were alerted about the fire, they implemented their disaster recovery plan. Within two days, they had the entire EMR system functioning at the satellite office. None of Nili's data was lost in the fire. As a matter of fact, we didn't lose any patient data, even though the whole office burned down."

Chris picked it up again. "It seemed like business as usual when Nili had her appointment that week at the satellite office. We got her medicine that very day. I don't even want to think about how long it would have taken to get her results if the tests had actually been lost."

The focus group continued for about another forty minutes. People shared stories and made suggestions. Dr. Vitale asked them questions. They discussed not only how to improve the EHR system, but also how to improve the patient experience in general. The conversation gradually veered into specifics Sam couldn't follow. More than once, though, he found himself asking why he hadn't thought of this before. Not the EHR system—he'd never heard of them, so he couldn't have thought of them. But focus groups weren't a bad idea, either. After all, if patients aren't happy, they go elsewhere. And a practice that loses too many patients goes out of business.

Dr. Vitale thanked everyone for participating and closed the meeting. Parents and fidgety children moved quickly to the door. Once they were all gone, Sam and Dr. Vitale walked to a coffee station set in an alcove off a hallway. The doctor made himself a cup of tea, and Sam decided to get some coffee for the drive back home.

"It sounds like those backup servers really saved the practice after the fire," Sam said, more to make conversation than anything else.

"Absolutely. Chris was right—without that backup, I don't know how long it would have taken us to get back up to speed. But there was another factor, too."

"What's that?"

"Our firecracker practice administrator, Aviva, at the satellite office. She took the added appointments and workload totally in stride. She's really taken this whole EHR system and turned it into an art form. Dr. Taylor tried to get her to transfer here to the main office, but she wasn't interested. She lives in Winsted, and she can walk to work there."

"Really?" Sam had stopped stirring his coffee.

Dr. Vitale noticed Sam's surprise, but misinterpreted it. "Yes. People do still walk, y'know."

"She's a practice administrator who's made that much of a mark with an EHR system? I should probably talk to her."

"Would you like an introduction?"

'Jackpot!' thought Sam. "That would be wonderful."

On his way out of Taylor Pediatrics, with fresh coffee in his hand and Aviva's phone numbers in his pocket, Sam turned on his phone and accessed his voicemail.

"Hey, Sam! It's Karen. Just wanted to let you know that my small group sessions won't be going on as long as we originally thought. It looks like I'll be heading home a few days early."

"GAHH!" Sam tried to shake off the hot coffee that now covered his hand and sleeve. He had just barely caught his phone before it hit the pavement. When he put it back up to his ear, Karen's message was still playing.

"... to hear how your research is going. I want to have a meeting with you first thing as soon as I get back. This is really important, so I hope you're giving it your all. Bye-bye!"

Sam's head now throbbed more than his hand did. A few days early and a surprise meeting? The stakes had just been raised.

Chapter 11
The Practice Administrator

Sam was now a man on a mission. The more he learned about EHR systems, the more he felt he needed to know. Earlier in his journey, he had been reluctant to inconvenience anyone with his search for EHR information. Now, though, a combination of wanting to save his job and needing to make sure he understood all the ins and outs of EHR as quickly as possible led him to set aside his earlier hesitation.

So, with this renewed determination, Sam called Aviva to see how soon she could meet with him. Luckily, she had already planned on working late that evening. She gave him directions to the office.

Next he called The EHR Guru to see if they had completed their technology assessment at MedOne as scheduled. He was relieved to find out their onsite work was done and the report was about to be written. When Sam told him of Karen's earlier-than-expected return, the Guru agreed to accelerate the schedule and have the report completed by Tuesday.

Finally, he called Alina to tell her that he would once again be missing dinner at home.

What passes for the evening rush on route 44 in northwest Connecticut was fading away when Sam made the drive from Sharon to Winsted. He parked at the curb in front of a three-story Victorian house on a residential street just behind the main drag. He climbed the steps next to the "Taylor Pediatrics" sign, crossed the porch, and tried the door. It was locked. He looked for a doorbell or buzzer, but couldn't see one. He knocked.

"Hello?" he called out uncertainly.

A voice came back through the door. "Yeah! Wait a minute, Sam."

The door was opened by a petite, attractive woman in her mid-thirties. "Come on back! Last door on your left. I just have to finish something." And she dashed off as quickly as she had appeared.

Taylor Pediatrics' Torrington office was in a modern medical complex, and this building had obviously been built as someone's home but, even so, Sam noticed some similarities between the two offices. There was the same Lego table and several coloring books stacked neatly on their shelves. There was no dinosaur on the receptionist's desk, but it was neat and absent of any papers or files.

Sam turned into the hallway, but Aviva had already disappeared. When he stepped into her office, she was staring intently at her computer screen. Without even looking up, she motioned him to a seat opposite her desk.

"Hi Sam! Sorry, just give me ... a moment. I was trying to get ... this ... finished before you came."

"No problem."

Sam looked around. Besides the computer, Aviva's desk was populated by several picture frames and a fern. Another plant sat on a bookshelf, and a poster of a Fender guitar hung on the wall.

"Just about there ... Done!"

She stood up quickly and shook Sam's hand. "Hi Sam, I'm Aviva, it's nice to meet you. Go ahead and throw your coat over the chair back there."

"Likewise," Sam said. "Meeting you, I mean. Not, y'know, the coat." He felt he wasn't getting off to a good start. Aviva couldn't weigh more than ninety pounds, but she was a powerhouse. Sam was still trying to regain his balance.

Once Sam's coat was deposited and they'd both sat back down, Aviva put her elbows on the desk and leaned in toward him. "So, your practice is about to take the deep plunge into EHR systems. That right?"

Sam smiled. "That's correct. And I'm the one who's been selected to jump first, under threat of court martial." How many metaphors could he mix at once?

Aviva laughed. "I remember the feeling. Like you're at the top of a cliff, about to step over the edge, not even knowing where the bottom is?"

"Something like that, yeah."

"I'm excited for you."

Sam cocked an eyebrow. "Really? Why's that?"

"Because, one: You're actually making the jump. And two: Once you jump, you'll learn how to fly."

"I like flying."

"Sam, I can rattle off a dozen reasons why our EHR system has been a help to me as a practice administrator."

Sam pulled out his pad and pen. "I'm all ears."

"Alright. First I want you to notice this picture right here." She turned around one of the frames so it faced him.

"It looks like a giraffe made from noodles."

"Correct! My son made it for me. He's only in second grade and already quite the artist! Before we got our EHR, I couldn't put a coffee mug down on my desk, much less mount a piece of artwork. I had piles of superbills, transcriptions, charts, you name it. As many as I could get done in one day, more would show up the next."

Sam nodded. She could have been describing his desk.

"Now the EHR system determines the coding. It even guides the doctor to optimize the coding in accordance with accepted medical practice."

Sam liked the idea of less coding in his life. He could still recite some of the more common codes he used when working for his dad over the summers.

"The doctors dictate their visit notes into the system. Boom! No more transcription costs. Or filing. No data entry required by me or the billing staff."

"I hadn't thought about billing." Was there any part of the practice an EHR system didn't affect?

"When the doctor enters the diagnoses and procedures, the associated fees are calculated on the form automatically. We no longer pull charts, 'cause all the patients' records are in the system. And if we need hard copy for some reason, we just print it out. You want to talk money?"

"Uhh ... sure." He was getting whiplash trying to keep up with the twists and turns in her conversation.

"In the seven years since we implemented the system, we've saved over one and a half million dollars. We had a net increase of one million dollars, due to increased patient volume. But we haven't had to hire any additional billing staff. Heck, we reduced our full-time billing staff by five employees. We also save about three thousand dollars a year in charts and supplies."

"Wait." Sam wanted to backtrack a bit. "You increased patient volume and decreased your billing staff? But more patients mean more bills and claims to submit and process."

"Absolutely. But the EHR system streamlines the entire billing process. It has rules about how to bill certain insurance companies. That feature has increased our first-pass pay rate up to roughly ninety-nine percent."

Sam was impressed. He'd never heard of a rate that high.

"We submit the claims to the insurance companies instantly. Overnight, we can view the status of the claims through our clearinghouse portal. When a claim is either paid or rejected, we can see it updated automatically on our account. So we're not constantly making calls to see if a claim has gone through or been lost."

Aviva started ticking off items on her fingers. "Our email has been linked into the system. Our fax line has been linked to the system. Our iPads and iPhones have been linked into the system."

"But what happens if the system goes down?"

She paused, but only for a moment. "About nine months ago, our main office—"

"I know. And a fire is catastrophic, but it's rare." Sam felt he was taking his life in his hands by interrupting Aviva, but he survived. "How often have servers gone down just because of being overworked or bad wiring or something like that? And with all those functions hooked into the same system, wouldn't it hobble the practice if it went down?"

If Aviva was upset about being interrupted, she didn't show it. She just grabbed the new topic and plowed on again at full speed.

"About two years ago, a member of the Guru's team was upgrading some software. Oh, sorry. The EHR Guru is—"

"I know who he is."

"Cool. So the guy's in here installing software, and the system goes down. He hadn't done anything wrong. A part had failed on the server. Not his fault. It was about eight o'clock at night. The tech called his CTO at home for advice." Sam decided to figure out what a CTO was later. "Then he loaded the server into his car and drove back to their office in Queens. A couple of spare parts and a few hours of work, and he gets the thing fixed. Then he met another member of their technical team who drove the server back here to the office. The second guy installed it and ran a full battery of tests before daybreak. They literally worked around the clock so the next day our office systems were up and running.

"And get this: I wasn't even aware there'd been a problem until that afternoon when they called to tell me. And I run everything around here!"

Sam whistled. If a computer at MedOne died, it would usually take somewhere between two days and a week to find a replacement. Then reloading the system with all their data would take at least another day. Aviva's story was impressive, but something about it bothered him. "That must have cost you a bundle."

Aviva shook her head. "Replacement parts. Everything else was covered under our service plan. We pay The EHR Guru a fair amount for service and support, but they earn it. The Guru takes full responsibility for keeping our systems functioning. He hasn't let us down yet. And speaking of money ..."

Sam's head jerked up. Were they speaking of money? Still? Again?

"... if you can qualify for Meaningful Use, and frankly—"

Once again, Sam felt as if he were stepping in front of a speeding train. "Could you explain that to me?"

"Meaningful Use?"

"Yes, please."

"Sure. Meaningful Use is .... Well, I'm not sure what it is. I guess it's the government wanting to make sure you're not taking their money and screwing around with it. You just have to show you're actually using the EHR system. They've got a list of fifteen things you have to swear you did—they call them "objectives." Then there's another list of ten things, and you have to prove you did five of them.

"But Sam, they're mostly basic things. I mean, they vary from specialty to specialty, so yours will be a little different from ours. But still—'Submit Prescriptions Electronically.' 'Maintain Medication Allergy List.' If you've got an EHR system and you're not doing these things, there's something wrong with you. Heck, they don't even make you do it all the time, just for a certain percentage of your patients. We do it for all our patients because, y'know, why wouldn't you?"

Sam looked down at his scrawls on the yellow, lined paper.

"Hey," Aviva continued, "Y'know what? I think I read they're going to increase the requirements soon. Guess you'd better move fast, Sam!"

Chapter 12
The Technology Assessment

"Sam, our assessment indicates that MedOne has quite a bit of work to do."

It was Monday evening, and Sam was once again sitting in the conference room, across the table from the Guru. He had ended up spending more than two hours with Aviva, discussing EHR systems from a practice administrator's point of view. That meeting had gone so well that Sam had been able to relax (a little) and enjoy a quiet weekend with Alina and Kevin. In the office Monday morning, the Guru had called to say the technology assessment report would be ready ahead of schedule. Sam made an appointment for the end of that day.

Now he was back at the conference table in Queens. Dozens of framed certifications stared down from the wall behind him as he flipped through one of several copies of a report with the words MedOne Technology Assessment typed on the cover, just above The EHR Guru's now-familiar power-button-and-caduceus logo.

"We identified a number of significant technology issues," the Guru continued, "but I'm confident that once these are remediated, MedOne will have a successful EHR implementation and realize all the benefits you've seen at our clients' practices."

"Wow," said Sam, leafing through the pages. "This is pretty detailed. Your people got it done fast."

"They're good. I spent some time this afternoon going over it. In your copy, I highlighted a few particular sections that show some key technical issues you must improve in order to prepare MedOne to implement an EHR."

"Would you mind if we take it a little slow on the explanations?" Sam asked. "Trying to get the coffee pot to work in the mornings has given me headaches. My knowledge of IT jargon begins and ends with the word computer."

The Guru smiled. "Sure, that's no problem. In fact, why don't we take it easy today? Ask me whatever questions you have at this point, and I'll try to answer them. Then you can take a little time to work your way through the assessment—it's mostly written in plain English—and come back with whatever new questions you have."

"That would be great," sighed Sam. "Would you mind if I asked what procedures your gurus go through when they perform a technical analysis? I want to make sure that, when Karen asks about the guys exploring our offices, I have a good answer as to what they were doing."

"Certainly. We have a standard process we follow in order to get the best picture of the client's technology infrastructure. That's the term we use to refer to all technical equipment and service—'technology infrastructure.' The process can be divided into three general phases: Data collection, analysis and documentation, and recommendations.

"Today, just about every office uses some kind of technology, even if they are not using an EMR. At MedOne, for example, you use MedMast for billing and scheduling. It runs on an old Unix server with a few desktop computers and printers. MedOne also has a slow DSL internet connection through the phone company."

"I thought DSL was a high-speed connection."

The Guru smiled. "At one time it was."

"Oh."

"In phase one," he continued, "we collect the technical details of everything in your office including computers, servers, software, network devices, communication devices, internet services, lab services, phone and fax services, key business applications, and network cables. The last time you were here, we talked about uptime. Uptime is vital to a successful EHR implementation. One critical component in the determination of uptime is the stability of the technical infrastructure in your office.

Sam was expecting the worst. "Okay, and how are we doing?"

"To be honest, Sam, there are quite a few places where your network could be improved, including that mess of cables and switches in the coat closet. But you'll see that once you reach the recommendations section of the report."

Sam's thoughts jumped to the staff coat closet at MedOne, with its spider's nest of network cables tangled with the coat hangers. He remembered how one winter's day last year, the practice had lost all phone service and access to their practice management server. After hours of frantic calls to the phone company, Sam had given up and called Izzy, a local "computer guy" and friend of Karen's. Izzy had found that the heavy winter coats all crammed together had caused a central switch in the closet to shut down. It was a simple matter to fix, but the downtime and lost communications had been harrowing.

"In addition to reviewing the practice's workflow, we also conduct interviews with employees to determine their current experiences with your existing technology. If the same issues and inefficiencies are mentioned in several different interviews, or the same technology upgrades appear on several different user wish lists, then we know those are areas and ideas we should look into more closely.

"But we don't limit ourselves to technical issues in the data-collection phase. We also review the management goals and strategic business plans of the practice. For example, Sam, do you know where Karen would like to eventually install a staff lounge?"

Sam was confused. "I wasn't aware of any plans to do that. I mean, we don't really have the space for it."

"Really? There's no small back room that's out of the way from the regular hustle and bustle of the practice? No little nook that is otherwise presently preoccupied with leaning towers of paperweight?"

Sam gasped. "The supply room? She said that?"

The Guru flicked a finger across the screen of his iPad. "Yes. According to someone named Emily, she did. It was in a management wish list for this upcoming year. I'd imagine that room would seem a lot bigger if all the charts and forms suddenly disappeared.

"This is a very minor example of the types of changes we at The EHR Guru try to be aware of so we can help our clients achieve their goals—even goals that don't directly relate to the adoption of an EHR system. And it's one of the biggest benefits of working with my team. We share a key skill with your physicians, Sam. We know the right questions to ask. When a doctor doesn't ask the right questions, they can misdiagnose the cause of a patient's health issue. In a similar way, because we ask the insightful diagnostic questions throughout the assessment process, we can correctly diagnose your technical challenges and recommend solutions that heal your practice."

"So should I be calling you 'Dr. Guru'?"

The Guru laughed. "If we're going to work together, Sam, we should be on a first-name basis with each other."

"So I should call you 'The.'"

"That's good," he said, laughing even harder. "I'll have to remember that one."

"So is that it for the data-collection phase?"

"Not quite. Communication services, such as internet and telephone service, are another facet we examine. During the assessment, we review in detail all the bills our clients receive, both to document the specific services in use and to see if we can find any cost savings. For instance, we found we were able to reduce one client's internet charges thirty-three percent simply by asking their service provider for a lower rate. As technology changes, internet rates are often reduced, but you won't get the lower rate unless you ask. Another client was paying for monthly communication services they had stopped using two years prior to our visit. They'd just forgotten to notify the service provider that they'd changed companies. It's common for us to save new clients thousands of dollars annually by helping them more wisely choose certain services.

Sam was actually retaining more information than he thought he would. "Alright, but why are you looking at everything? MedOne is contracting you—maybe—to help us implement and use an EHR system. Why do you care about all the other systems in the office?"

"Excellent question. Because Sam, the faster, more streamlined, and more stable a practice's data network, communications and infrastructure are, the smoother the adoption of an EHR system will be."

Sam sat back, satisfied with the answer. "So, phase two now?"

"Yes. Analysis and documentation. Once our gurus collect all of the necessary information on-site, they come back to our office to analyze and document their findings using technical diagrams and tables. We then review these issues with our team of system engineers. We brainstorm the costs and benefits of various recommendations until we arrive at a consensus. These become the final recommendations included in your assessment.

"Alright," said Sam, "let's break down some of those issues and recommendations. I want to make sure I understand them."

The Guru flipped through his copy of the report, looking at section headings. "'Areas to Improve Work Flow' is a somewhat broad category. It's any factor having to do with the system that is potentially slowing down productivity. Let me give you a technical example. After analyzing the hard drive partitions on many of your servers, we found that the majority of them are close to capacity. Low disk space can adversely affect the performance and stability of these servers. We've also discovered that many of the computer service packs are outdated and hardware warranties have expired. Keeping your systems up to date is vital to maintaining stability, security, and performance."

"And uptime," Sam chimed in.

"That's right. Your new EHR system needs a secure, stable, and fast environment to perform well. It's also not possible to support very old equipment, and not cost-effective to diagnose problems, when they inevitably occur, with such equipment.

"My team also considers the internal procedures within your company. These can be strictly manual processes, or processes that combine technology with human interaction. We compare this to the best practices we have identified at the most efficient medical offices in the country and make recommendations on how you can improve. At one practice, we recommended they use this orange tablet computer for patients to fill out their intake forms. The tablet computer is free, and the practice gets a legible document that can be automatically uploaded into the EHR."

"Free tablet computers? Can I have one? Only, in silver, not orange."

"We'll see."

"Oh, man! I'm a dad. I know that 'we'll see' means 'no.'"

Sam was surprised to hear himself joking like this, especially with someone he really didn't know very well. He realized that his mood was lighter than it had been in ... well, it felt like weeks. He credited it to the Guru. The report in front of him might or might not hold the answers to all of Sam's problems. But the man across from him seemed to know that it would. He exuded an air of confidence and competence that lifted the weight off Sam's shoulders.

"Finally, there's the mismatching of tools and users. Here we look for incompatibilities between users and the tools at their disposal. For instance, you might have a computer that is not fast enough for a user to get their work done quickly. Another common issue is companies buying technology because it seems like a 'deal' rather than because it truly meets their needs. At MedOne, we found that you do not have two printers or scanners that are the same model. This increases your support costs because you have to learn the little configuration tricks and tweaks required for each model work optimally. In addition, if one breaks down, you won't be able to swap the devices or parts with another one already in the office."

This was not news to Sam. Just last week, they had run out of toner for the HP laser printer at the front desk. He had tried to use a toner cartridge from the HP printer in his own office, but they were different models and not compatible. Patients had left without their usual receipts while someone made an emergency Staples run.

"Phase three is recommendations, which are clearly set out in the technology assessment report. I suggest we stop here to give you time to review the report on your own. If I keep talking, you might feel like you're drinking water from a fire hose."

"It feels that way already," Sam replied with a laugh.

"I'm very interested in going over the full results of the assessment with you and Karen. But considering your situation, it's probably best that you first fully comprehend our assessment and recommendations. After Karen returns, we can schedule a meeting with the two of you, and perhaps other members of your practice as well. Then one of my lead engineers and I can walk you through all the details."

Sam nodded. "I'm pretty sure we will be moving ahead with an EHR system, but she's the primary decision-maker."

The Guru started rummaging for something in his desk drawers. "I'm going to give you the information for one of our most experienced software technicians." The Guru offered Sam a card. "As I said, the recommendations are mostly in plain English, but I'm sure you will have additional questions. If you can't reach me, please don't hesitate to reach out to Aleem Khordashi. He is the lead consultant who wrote your technology assessment report."

Sam took the card and slipped it into his pocket as he stood up. "Everything sounds great. I know you're busy, so I'll contact Aleem with my questions. And thank you very much for making our schedule a priority."

The Guru rose to meet him and they shook hands. "You're welcome. It would be an honor to work with you and serve your organization. I look forward to our next conversation!"

As he walked out of The EHR Guru's building, Sam could feel his stress level increasing again. So much would be riding on the meeting with Karen once she got back. Which was why it was so important that Sam continue to learn as much about EHR as possible. Back in his car, before he even started the ignition, Sam had his cell phone in his hand.

Chapter 13
Selecting EHR Software and A Technology Partner

Sam was hungry. That term is often used to describe someone who wants to get ahead in his career. As far as Sam was concerned, he wasn't trying to get ahead, he was just trying not to get fired. Today, Sam was just plain hungry. He'd skipped lunch and needed food.

It was Tuesday, and Karen was due back in three days. Sam had read through the MedOne technology assessment report and had actually understood just about all of it. But there were still some things he felt he needed to know more about. That was why he was meeting Aleem Khordashi at Rosie's Café, just down the street from the MedOne offices. The food at Rosie's was a bonus.

Once Sam entered the restaurant, Aleem was not hard to spot. He had no tie, but he was wearing a suit, and he was the only one in the restaurant who was. And then there was the rolling computer case parked next to him. Sam walked over.

"Aleem?"

"Sam?" inquired the man, as he stood and offered his hand.

Sam shook it. "It's nice to meet you."

"You as well." Aleem was about forty, with a kind, round face and not a lot of hair.

"Can I get you anything to drink or a snack?" Sam asked.

"I'm good, thanks." He pointed to his cup on the table.

"Just give me a moment." Sam went to the counter and ordered his liquid caffeine and a sandwich. He joked with Rose—who hated being called Rosie, even though that's what she'd named the restaurant—as she made the sandwich. Once he was supplied and paid up, he joined Aleem at the table.

Aleem started. "I figure you may have a number of questions based on your technology assessment, but if it's okay with you, let's step back for a moment so you understand my background. I have an advantage in this conversation because the Guru gave me a full background on you. I've studied your business, whereas all you know is that I work for the Guru."

"As a senior consultant, I know that, too." It was the job title on Aleem's business card.

"I've been working in IT as an engineer, project manager, and consultant for over fifteen years. I've worked for the Guru for about the last six years. We met on a project where the software company I was working for had done a poor job of implementing an EHR system and the Guru was called to fix it. I was so impressed with the work he did that I asked him for a job. I love what I do, and I'm happy to help you any way I can."

Sam liked the way that sounded. "Okay. How about we start by you telling me about choosing an EHR software system?"

"Alright. Let's talk software in general terms at first, rather than the specific recommendations in your technology assessment report. The first thing to know is there is no one-size-fits-all solution. Each practice or hospital must select the program they believe best satisfies their key operational and clinical requirements. Obviously, these are often unique to the type of practice or healthcare network. Everyone is different, everyone's needs are different, and you have to match your needs to what's on the market.

"Of course, this assumes that the practice or hospital has even taken the time to identify their key requirements. We find that many EHR implementations fail with this first critical step. You have to reach a consensus across your organization as to what the organization's key requirements are."

Sam realized that would have to be the topic of a meeting—probably several meetings—between himself, Karen, and Jack Kohn, Karen's second-in-command at the practice. And maybe all the partners as well.

Aleem gestured to the blackboard hanging over the counter. "You can compare software selection to that menu. Lots of the items up there would satisfy my desire to no longer be hungry. But since I have celiac disease, only some of them will satisfy my need to not have any gluten in my diet. A dish of ice cream might be a short-term solution, but if I'm trying to lose weight, it doesn't meet my long-term needs. It's important that I make a wise choice."

Sam realized he should be taking notes. He opened his briefcase and took out his iPad.

"Sam, I think you've been undersold to me."

"Sorry?"

"I was told you were a technophobe."

Sam shrugged and gave an embarrassed grin. "It was an anniversary present from my wife."

He didn't mention that their anniversary had been four months earlier, or that he had hardly turned the thing on before last night. With all of his research into high-tech systems, Sam had started to become less afraid of technology and more comfortable experimenting with some of the gadgets his more tech-savvy colleagues used.

For some reason, Aleem appeared pleased to see Sam working with the iPad. "Good for you," he said. "Now, during the evaluation of your new system, there are some key actions to avoid. The first is being a pioneer with a new EHR system. EHRs have been around long enough that you don't need to go through the time, hassle, and lost productivity involved with serving as a test site. One of the simplest qualifications to consider is whether practices similar to yours in size and/or specialty are using the software successfully.

"Another thing to avoid is adding clinical content for your specialty to the product's existing features. I've seen cases where in-house IT departments have tried to get a little overly creative by building out so many custom templates and interfaces that they had difficulty getting support on the product."

"Being overly creative with technology's never really been a problem for me."

Aleem laughed. "You also want to make sure the EHR system you're purchasing has been certified by one of the six ONC-authorized certifying organizations." Sam opened his mouth, but Aleem answered the question before he could ask it. "The Office of the National Coordinator for Health Information Technology. It oversees the definition and certification of Meaningful Use. This endorsement is important because one of the foundations of Meaningful Use is to use a certified EHR. But there's another benefit to certification that's not as obvious. The requirements are rigorous, so having certification typically indicates the vendor has both the staying power and the financial resources to continually invest in their product."

Sam was trying to balance the iPad on his thigh, type on it, and eat his sandwich, all at the same time. It wasn't going well.

"Certification. Got it. Tell me more things I shouldn't do."

"Most practices we work with have been using some sort of computerized practice management system for billing and scheduling for many years. Since they are so comfortable using this system, some clients want to continue to use their PM system while integrating it with a new EMR system from some other software vendor."

"Not a good idea?"

"We don't recommend it for so many reasons."

"Just name one."

"The user interfaces will be very different, and therefore confusing when you shift back and forth. Also the difficulty of keeping all required data synchronized between the two systems."

"That's two."

"I hope you can forgive me."

Sam grinned as he reached back for his coffee, which was on the empty table behind him. The food at Rosie's was good, but the tables were small.

"Also," Aleem continued, "make sure to have your doctors and key support staff preview or demo the systems during your evaluation process. It's important that a few of your key people actually sit at workstations and experience the software. You want to be sure they're comfortable with its navigation, administrative features, reports, and ease of use."

Sam remembered his own experience at the workstation with Nurse Gabe. "Good idea."

"Typically we help our clients find software that reinforces the best practices and workflows of their offices. That way your people are able to learn the software faster and it reinforces your culture and clinical focus."

"Alright, hold on," Sam looked up. "What do you mean by 'culture with your clinical focus'?"

"What I mean is, will the selected EHR program support how your doctors and staff currently interact with your patients? You can select the best program in the world, but if it drastically changes workflow without improving the way your doctors and staff care for patients, then the implementation is a step backwards in patient care and will most likely fail."

"Are you saying we can avoid a learning curve?"

Aleem shook his head. "There's always a learning curve with all software. But there's a difference between learning how to use the software and changing the way your office runs in order to accommodate the software. You should choose a program that already works the way you do."

The explanation sparked a question in Sam's head. "Have you had any clients who have ultimately rejected the system they purchased?"

Aleem paused before answering. "No. I can't think of any time I've heard of a practice uninstalling a system and going back to the way they'd been doing things before." He took a sip of what looked to Sam like tea. "But I do know of EHR systems installed by other companies that have languished and never been fully implemented. And we've been called in many times to turn around a failing implementation. That's how I met the Guru in the first place, remember?" He took another sip and set the cup back down. "We've helped clients who had inadequate systems upgrade to software, networks, and other technology that better met their needs. But on installs we manage ourselves, we have a one-hundred-percent success rate."

Sam sat back in his chair. "So, not to toot your own horn, but you guys don't make any mistakes."

Aleem smiled. "Everybody makes mistakes. The key is how well you resolve them and move beyond them." He thought a second. "Actually, the key is how well you avoid mistakes in the first place. Then, when a few, inevitable mistakes occur, the key is how well you resolve them and move beyond them."

Sam popped the last bite of sandwich into his mouth, set the plate aside, and placed the iPad on the table in front of him. He spoke around the sandwich. "So, what you're saying is the selection of a technology partner is just as important as the selection of an EHR system."

"Absolutely. Not to be too dramatic, but the entire success or failure of an EHR implementation may depend on the technology partner you select."

"So what should I look for when choosing a partner? Besides your name on the payroll, I mean."

Aleem smiled to show he hadn't taken offense. "Sam, I'm a software technician. I'm not in the sales department. I think you should look at other technology partners. Ask questions, make comparisons. We can stand up to the scrutiny."

Sam was impressed. "Fair enough. So what should I look for?"

"One key factor is to make sure the company has at least five years' experience installing and supporting EHR systems. No matter how much experience they have in other areas of technology, an EHR system is a unique animal. Hiring a company without experience in EHR implementation project management is like going to an OB/GYN instead of an orthopedist for a knee replacement."

"Ouch," Sam winced.

"You said it. Check on the company's support system as well. How well do they remotely monitor your network and the other technology you've implemented? How many techs are available for support, and what are their support hours?"

"In case there's an emergency."

"Yes, but not just that. It's simply not possible to perform maintenance on an EHR system during the day while doctors are seeing patients. So it's critical your technology partner has enough staff to work nights and weekends to perform preventive maintenance activities." He paused a moment to let Sam's note-taking catch up. "One final consideration in evaluating an IT support group is the business continuity plan they recommend to be used in the event of a system crash."

"What's that?"

"It's a straightforward, step-by-step process to be followed immediately after a disaster in order to avoid technical failures and restore the technology that supports your business."

"Oh, right," said Sam quickly. "I heard about what you guys did after the fire."

"Which fire?"

"You've had more than one?"

"We haven't had any, but several of our clients have. We have a lot of clients, Sam."

"And they were all up and running the next day?"

"No. One took two days"

Sam stopped to think a minute. "Let me play devil's advocate a minute. Say my boss decides she wants to save money on this project. What's stopping us from just purchasing what we think is the best system, installing it, and learning it ourselves?"

Aleem smiled. "Nothing. And you'll think you are saving money, at first. But like the person who gets the knee replacement from the OB/GYN, you're going to have problems. And those problems will distract you from your primary task, which is serving your patients. In the end, it will cost you far more than just engaging a quality IT-support organization to help you in the first place.

"Think about it. Who in your organization has prior experience with an EHR system, is ready to properly teach it to your staff and doctors, and will be on-call twenty-four-seven to monitor the system in case anything goes wrong, and be ready, able, and willing to fix it?"

"Hmm. I see your point."

"That's just a few of the issues. There are plenty more. Having the technical knowledge is an incredibly important factor for your technology partner to have, but it may not be your most important consideration."

"Really? What would?"

"Credibility might be one of, if not the, most important criteria. The companies actually worth your time will be the ones who can refer you to their clients as character references. You need to do exactly what you're doing now. Talk with their clients and ask the hard questions. Visit offices, check out systems. See if they serve their clients the way you want MedOne to serve its patients."

Aleem looked down at his watch. "Wow, looks like I need to hit the road. Do you have any other questions you need answered right now? We can meet again or talk by phone if you have more to discuss."

"Well, I'm going to have to explain to my boss how the implementation process works. I hate to ask you to make a long business call in the evening ..."

"I don't mind." Aleem unzipped his computer bag and pulled out a slick laptop computer. "But as it happens, I have a better idea. How would you like to see part of an implementation in action?"

"Yes! That would be great!"

Aleem was typing already. "I'm sending you an email with the information for one of our clients. We're finalizing the implementation process for their system this week. They're a small hospital in Danbury. Are you familiar with Grace Presbyterian?"

Sam nodded and smiled. "We've actually had a few references come from there over the years. I know some of their staff."

"Wonderful! Then it should be easier for you to be part of their meeting. There. We're all set." He shut the computer down again. "We'll be having a series of meetings with them this week. You can go ahead and pick which one you would like to attend."

Sam thought about his impending deadline. "Are there any scheduled for tomorrow?"

"Yes."

"I'll be there."

As they walked out of the coffee shop, the two men said their goodbyes and got into their cars. Sam felt a growing excitement. This upcoming meeting would enable him to see the Guru's team in action during a real EHR implementation. He smiled and wondered whether he had a guardian angel watching over him. He had been incredibly busy since Karen left, but he could not remember a time when he'd been more productive. Just before he turned the key, he quietly said, "Thanks."

Chapter 14
The EHR Implementation

When he walked into Grace Presbyterian the next morning, Sam remembered why he had such an affinity for this particular hospital. Numerous trees and lawns dotting the front entrance, full-length glass panes enclosing the main lobby, pastel designs on the carpet, and even an indoor waterfall gave the place a feel more reminiscent of a university or health club than a hospital.

After informing the nurse at the front desk that he was with the Guru's team, Sam was directed to a conference room located up the stairs and to the left. As he walked down the second-floor hallway, a man sitting in a chair opposite the conference room door stood up to meet him. He was short and skinny and had a professorial air about him.

"Hi. Can I help you?"

"Yes, my name's Sam Bushman. I'm here to join a meeting with The EHR Guru and Grace management?"

"Oh, yes! My name's Joseph Eng. I'm one of the engineers from The EHR Guru assigned to Grace Presbyterian. Please call me Joe."

"Nice to meet you, Joe." They shook hands.

"You as well. The meeting won't start for a few minutes, but I've been charged with bringing you up to speed prior to going in. That way you'll understand what this meeting is going to be about."

"Wonderful."

Joe led Sam down the hall and around a corner. After talking a bit about their mutual backgrounds, Joe got down to business.

"So, from what Aleem told me, you're new to EHR systems, and this will be the first implementation meeting you've ever participated in. Is this correct?"

"Yep. And I have so many questions. How did Grace decide which EHR system to go with?"

"I don't know. What we're doing here is upgrading a system they put in place a few years ago. They hired us to install new technology to augment the system, design improved workflows, train their people, and support the system on an ongoing basis. Now we're transferring data from their former system to the upgrade in addition to our other work. Data conversion between systems is a whole project by itself."

"Well, all we have now is MedMast. We'll have to install a new system from scratch." Sam was worried this meeting might turn out to be a waste of his time. And he didn't have a lot of time.

It was almost as if Joe had read his mind. "Okay. But this meeting will still have value for you because we follow a similar process whether we're implementing a brand-new EHR system or helping a client optimize an existing one."

"Oh, good. So what it is that process?"

"The first three phases of our implementation process are managed as part of our technology assessment. I assume you've at least looked over your technology assessment report. Do you remember what those three phases are?"

Sam felt like a kid being called on in class. "I believe they are data gathering, data analysis, and recommendations."

"Right! These were completed a few months ago. Then about six weeks ago, Aleem and other members of The EHR Guru fulfilled the fourth phase by presenting these findings and recommendations to the project team here at Grace."

"So phase four is presenting the report?"

"Yes."

"Jeez, the Guru just handed me a copy."

Joe smiled patiently. "That wasn't phase four. At some point in the near future, we'll schedule a meeting with one or two of our engineers, you, and some of the doctors from your practice."

Now Sam remembered that the Guru had mentioned that at the end of their meeting. "Yeah, I knew that."

Joe continued, "Based upon the results of our meeting with the Grace team, including the feedback we got from management, we followed through with the fifth phase. Want to guess?"

"Ummmm ... Implementation?"

"Close. But first we have to formulate an implementation plan. And that brings us to today's meeting, where Aleem and other members of the team are presenting the implementation plan to the project team. We'll all review and discuss it together. That's phase six."

Sam whistled. "That sounds like a lot of work. How many phases do you guys have, anyway?"

"The amount of work varies depending on the size of the organization, the current technology they're using, the efficiency of their work processes, stuff like that. And all told, there are eight phases. The seventh phase is the actual implementation of the plan, and the eighth is the ongoing review and maintenance of the system."

"How long does phase eight take?"

"It lasts for as long as you use the system and your practice is contracted with us. We're constantly evaluating our procedures and systems. We want to be sure we're providing the best-possible experience for our clients." Joe looked at his watch. "Do you have any other questions?"

Sam shook his head. "No. Is it time to go in?"

"We should."

When Sam and Joe entered the conference room, all conversation stopped, and eight pairs of eyes turn toward them. An older man in a lab coat stopped talking to Aleem and strode over to Sam.

"Well, look if it isn't old Mr. Bushman come to pay us a visit!" The doctor beamed as he locked Sam's hand in a hearty handshake.

Sam recognized the man, but couldn't quite come up with his name, and having everyone in the room staring at him wasn't helping him think. He smiled weakly but tried to speak confidently. "It's good to see you again! How've you been?"

This time, the man spoke softly. "You don't remember me, do you, Sam?"

"No, of course I do."

"That's alright!" He was loud and hearty once again. "My name's Dr. Eddy Mauer! Internist. I've sent quite a few patients over to you and Karen over the years. What are you doing down 'round these parts?"

Sam really wanted to stop being the center of attention in the room, so his response was as brief as he could make it. "Karen's decided it's time to improve the efficiency of our practice, and I'm researching ways to do that."

"Great! That's exactly what we're doing here. Have a seat!" Dr. Mauer motioned Sam to a chair as he went back to his side of the table. "Aleem's trying to help us improve our EHR system. Great software in concept, but we haven't gotten much out of our current solution because it has limited functionality." The way he said limited functionality, Sam could almost hear quotation marks around it. "We really need something more comprehensive, which is what we're implementin' now. Speaking of which, have you met—"

"Yes!" Aleem jumped in, trying to regain control of the meeting. "Sam and I had lunch together yesterday. Now, if everyone's ready, we can start."

"If it's alright," piped up one doctor who sat several seats to Dr. Mauer's left, "can we start with the recommendations first, and then go over the plan?" Sam wondered why this guy wanted to go back to phase four, when everyone else in the room was ready for phase six. Or was it seven?

"Certainly," Aleem assured him. "Let me summarize what our goals are for this project. As part of phase four, we determined that these were the three main goals for this assessment and implementation."

He hit a key on his laptop, and a slide appeared on the video screen on the front wall:

1. Improve the patient experience by better utilizing technology to access patient data faster, remind doctors and staff of medical and personal information relating to the patient, and improve workflows within the organization;

2. Train our people so they understand how fully utilizing this technology enables us to better serve patients and reinforces the unique culture of our organization; and

3. Implement this technology prudently in stages so our people are not overwhelmed by the changes and we have the training and support necessary to provide uninterrupted quality service to our patients.

"Are we in agreement with these three objectives?" Aleem asked, and received everyone's nod of approval.

Sam listened as Aleem explained their detailed recommendations for the overall EHR system implementation, general training and workflow design, and how the Guru's people would support the new system.

Sam thought of something and leaned over to Joe. "Does the hospital have to accept all of the recommendations you put forward?" he asked softly.

Joe shook his head. No, the project team can decide the ones they want to implement and others they want to pass over. But some recommendations build on one another, though."

"Such as?"

"Well, for example, in order to design custom clinical alerts based on lab results, you have to fully integrate the lab reporting directly into the EHR. You can't decide against integrated lab reporting and then ask for custom alerts."

Sam nodded and continued scanning the plan. When he finished, Aleem was saying, "At the conclusion of this meeting, we want to confirm the timeline to gain all the necessary approvals. Then we can move ahead with the project according to your schedule. This would move us to phase seven, the actual implementation of your new system."

The next hour consisted of lively discussions back and forth between the two groups as timetables for the project were defined, deliverables for the EHR system were refined, and required resources, such as a temporary training facility and workspace for the Guru employees at Grace, were discussed. Aleem also sought consensus for a key milestone called the "go-live" date. Sam realized this was the day on which the hospital would stop using their existing system and cut over to the new system.

As the meeting was coming to a close, Aleem summarized the group's next steps. "Thank you for the work you have done prior to this meeting to fully explore the needs of your organization, with us and with your people. We will incorporate the changes you've requested into our implementation plan and submit our proposal for approval within two business days. You've indicated we can expect to have everything signed-off on by the fifteenth of the month. Assuming that happens, we will schedule our people to begin work the following week and provide you with a specific, step-by-step project timeline so everyone is clear on the process we will be following."

Dr. Mauer nodded. "Thank you, Aleem. And Joe."

As hands were shaken and people started to file out, Sam put the implementation plan and his iPad into his briefcase. Joe went over to speak with Aleem. After a hushed conversation Sam couldn't quite hear, Joe came back with a smile on his face.

"Well, Sam, you're going to have to thank me someday."

"I'd like to thank you now. You and everyone at The EHR Guru have already been so helpful."

"We're not done helping you yet. I just talked it over with Aleem, and he agrees that you should speak with our director of client services. Here's why: You're considering why you need an EHR system, the implementation of a system, and its impact on various people. But this is not a one-time event. Remember phase eight?"

"It lasts for as long as we use the system."

"Exactly. So you also should gain some perspective on the support needs related to using an EHR system and how to keep everything current."

The light bulb above Sam's head lit up. "So 'client services' is your customer support department."

Aleem had wandered over. "That's right. Don't forget, the support you receive during the first few weeks after your EHR system goes live is critical to your success."

Sam realized that he'd talked about support with the Guru and with Aleem, in the focus group and with Aviva, but he hadn't spoken to anyone from the Guru's support staff. It was definitely something he should do. But he had only two days until Karen returned.

"Now tell me, Sam," Joe said, "could you make it to another meeting here at ten o'clock tomorrow morning?"

Chapter 15
EHR Support and Upgrades

Thursday. The day before K-Day. Sam's mind was racing as he approached the door to the same conference room inside Grace Presbyterian. He reached for the handle, then stopped himself. He preferred not to make an attention-grabbing entrance as he had yesterday.

Instead, he sat in the chair that Joe had been in the day before and began going through his briefcase. As he was reflecting on the irony of all the sheaves of notes he had collected in his search for a paperless system, the conference door swung open, and two Guru employees headed down the hall toward the stairs. Following them were several clusters of doctors, chatting among themselves. Sam waited for the flow to subside before he made his way inside.

He put his briefcase down in front of the same seat he'd occupied yesterday. Sitting at the end of the table at the other side of the room was a man in a sharp suit with red-and-blue Elvis Costello glasses. He looked up as Sam came in.

"Let me guess. Sam Bushman?"

Sam walked over to shake hands. "You're right! And you must be Jake Carmel?"

"I am indeed! Just completed a fun Q-and-A discussion about how best to maintain the hospital's new EHR systems so they can provide a better experience for their patients and improve workflow and productivity for their staff. Do I understand correctly that MedOne will be installing its first EHR system?"

Ignoring the fact that he had already claimed a seat, Sam sat down next Jake. "Well, that's the plan. I still have to meet with my head physician to sell her on the idea."

"And during that meeting, you need to be able to answer any conceivable question she might come up with."

Sam smiled ruefully. "Kind of, yeah. I've learned a lot about the implementation and the different aspects of an EHR system, but not as much about what happens after it's installed. I'm guessing that's my next important lesson, since we don't want to have our new system crashing once a month."

"Precisely. But that's not the only issue. I've found that once clients get comfortable with their systems, they want to use more and more of the EHR features. Get more and more out of it. Once they're used to using the computers and infrastructure to run the EMR system, they want to automate other office functions, too."

"And you provide those upgrades for your clients?"

"Sometimes it's upgrades. Sometimes it's something the system is already capable of. All we have to do is show folks how to make it happen."

Sam chuckled. "And I thought all you did was trouble-shooting."

"Actually, that's part of expanding your usage of your systems, too. As you push the system to its limits, there are always technical glitches or unexpected challenges. You don't want to face them alone. Do you have an in-house IT department?"

"Not ... really."

"'Not really'?"

"Well, when something technical goes wrong, if the person who discovers it can't fix it—which is always—then it usually falls to the receptionist or one of the doctors to try and figure it out. Then, when that doesn't work, we call a guy named Izzy."

"Izzy."

"Yeah. I think it's pretty cool, actually. I'd never met anyone who was really named 'Izzy.'"

"Hmmm." Jake stroked his red beard for a moment. "Sam, I think you need to consider a more permanent and comprehensive IT support solution. You need someone with the expertise and availability to take care of your EHR system. To react, sometimes immediately, when there's a problem. If I may use an analogy ..." Sam looked around for a menu board, or an OB/GYN holding an artificial knee. These Guru guys sure did like analogies. "... using an EHR system without anyone on call who knows how to support it is like driving a taxi for a living without having a mechanic. Sooner or later the taxi has a problem. Your business shuts down until it's fixed. That's not where you want to be."

Sam nodded. "Don't I know it."

"Great. So, an EMR system is a complex program with so many features, it wouldn't be possible to implement all aspects of any system at one time. Users require time and practice to learn how to use the system. They have to adapt their internal workflow to get the most benefit from the system."

"Okay, but here's what I don't get," Sam interrupted. "Here at Grace, they bought their EMR from HealthMed, right?" He had been doing a lot of research.

"Yes."

"And doesn't HealthMed provide training on its system to people who purchase it?"

"You're right, they do. Up to a point. EMR software trainers usually travel to a practice for a couple of weeks. They provide initial training and workflow adaptation. Once those trainers leave, the practice is generally left on its own."

"Actually, HealthMed has a help desk support line."

"Right again. They also offer some online training courses. But our experience has been that not everybody learns at the same pace. Also, concepts that may have originally been understood in the middle of intensive training are forgotten if they don't come up in practice right away. Or a new workflow that may have made sense during training no longer works when implemented in real life."

"And the software company doesn't help you with that." It wasn't a question. Sam knew the answer.

"Not after the training period is over. At least, not without charging extra. That's one of the things we're doing here at Grace. The hospital has no one person with sufficient knowledge of the HealthMed EMR to analyze the workflow issues and recommend or create new workflows."

"But for day-to-day stuff, they use HealthMed's help desk?"

"Yes. Occasionally, though, they'll hit a technical problem the HealthMed EMR support team can't solve right away. Honestly? Part of the problem is the users who report the problem aren't able to accurately describe the scope of the issue. So HealthMed EMR support is unable to understand exactly what's going on."

Sam thought this through. "So if HealthMed support can't handle it, the hospital calls you."

"Yes."

"Alright, so why do they use HealthMed support at all? Why wouldn't The EHR Guru just provide everything?"

Jake stroked his beard again. He seemed to do that when he was thinking. "If an EHR system were a building, you could consider The EHR Guru team as contractors. We monitor the building's structure to make sure it can withstand the elements. Make sure the heating and air conditioning work properly so people can work comfortably. Fix things that break, and do other work to make certain the building fully supports the people who are trying to work in it. But the tenants don't call us in to turn the lights on and off.

"Part of our job is to train clients to take care of the simple aspects of maintenance, system configuration and support. They can do this more cost effectively and quickly than our people. We focus on the more complicated needs of their system that require our highly trained and certified engineers."

"Are there any systems where your support and maintenance services are not required?" Sam asked.

"No. That would be penny-wise and pound-foolish, as the old saying goes. You might save a bit of money early on. But the downtime, lost productivity, and hassles you experience will cost your medical practice significantly more than any money you'd saved."

Sam nodded. "That's what I thought."

"Just consider some of the relatively common challenges. There are power surges that can take down equipment. Viruses that can crash a system. Compatibility issues with so many applications from different vendors attempting to coexist on a single workstation or server. Next time you visit our office, I can share with you a typical day in the life of our help-desk techs. See the types of issues they deal with daily. Your doctors are experts at what they do. We're experts at what we do. We do our job well so your physicians and staff can do what they've been trained to do."

"These days, patients expect their doctors to anticipate and proactively treat their health problems." Sam hoped that hadn't sounded too snotty.

"Our clients use The EHR Guru for the same reason. For instance, we install temperature monitors in our clients' server closets. They alert us to temperature levels that could damage the electronics. One client's temperature monitor alerted us on a Sunday night in August at one A.M. The room temperature exceeded the safe limit for their servers. We connected remotely— saw that the temperature had steadily been rising. We quickly shut down the servers that were still running. Then we woke up the senior partner of the practice to tell him what was happening. At seven o'clock that morning, one of our techs was at their office to meet the AC repair crew and turn the servers back on after the AC repairs were finished."

"You guys must be night owls. Aviva Scarpelli at Taylor Pediatrics told me about a late-night run you did for them."

Jake laughed out loud. "That was a while ago! Joseph Eng was the tech—I think you met him yesterday."

"Yes, I did."

"Joe was working at Taylor's main office, installing some of the latest upgrades—necessary firmware, BIOS updates on one of their servers. After everything was installed, Joe rebooted the server, but a totally separate issue occurred. One of the DIMM memory modules was diagnosed by the internal server diagnostic system to be defective. The server wouldn't boot. This resulted in some midnight diagnostics back at our offices. We resolved the issue using some spare memory modules we had lying around from another client's old server. But now we had a new challenge: How to return the server to our client before the office opened. I couldn't trust Joe to stay awake long enough to drive the server back up to Connecticut. So I woke up Alex, another Guru tech. He picked up the server at our office, took it back out, and connected it back into the system."

"Wow," exclaimed Sam. "I don't understand half of what you said, but that sounds like a rather hectic evening."

Jake laughed. "Alex was not very happy about that call. But all our techs know they may be called upon at any time to assist with any client issues."

"Maybe everyone would've been better off if you'd skipped the upgrades." Sam was joking, but Jake took the comment seriously.

"Some clients choose not to do the upgrades," he said. "I don't recommend that as standard policy. Upgrades and patches are released for a reason—to improve the security, stability, and performance of your systems. Also to fix bugs. Sometimes they add new features you might like. The Guru is a stickler on following best practices. That calls for keeping all systems current with all tested patches. In fact, I believe that the HIPAA security rules require that you keep your systems up-to-date with all available security patches. You'd be surprised how often clients call us with a workstation issue—some type of incompatibility or slow performance—we update their system with all the latest patches, and the problem's solved."

Sam recalled the time he'd hired an electrician because the GFCI outlet in the master bathroom had stopped working. The electrician had pushed the Reset button and left. "If I were the client, I'd feel pretty foolish."

"There are no foolish clients, Sam. Only foolish ... uhh ..." Sam waited. "Okay, I don't know where I was going with that. But seriously, Sam, never hesitate to call us if you need help with anything."

"Assuming I contract with you."

"Of course."

"But I have to say, it sounds like you guys have it covered."

Jake sat forward in his seat. "We've only talked about the support we offer to all of our clients. Beyond this basic level, we offer more sophisticated technical services such as detailed architecture audits, network documentation, virtualization, and disaster planning."

"Those all sound incredibly helpful, but unfortunately, I'm not exactly sure what they mean," replied Sam.

"That's no problem. Let's go over each one, starting with the architecture audit. We had a new client whose EHR software would freeze whenever someone ran a report. Not just the user running the report—all the users, locked up tight. We ran an audit of their servers and EMR program, identified where the bottleneck was, and provided guidance on a technology workaround. Now people run reports without any detrimental effects to other users.

"Regarding the network documentation, we have a client with five office locations; all with servers and networks to maintain. Our network documentation provides every device name, make and model number, IP address, serial number, and overall function. That helps facilitate faster support. All of our techs also carry cameras. They photograph all the server and networking equipment. Without this level of detail, it would require a significant amount of time to identify the problem, determine the specific equipment involved, and diagnose a solution."

"That documentation would literally just look like a chart of ones and zeroes to me," laughed Sam. "I wouldn't know where to begin with it."

"Don't worry. You don't really have to fully understand all of this. We encourage you to understand as much of the technical details as you wish. But this documentation really is for the techies.

Going back to our car and mechanic analogy, do you know what a carburetor looks like? No. But you can drive your car anyway."

"Thank goodness for that."

"What was next?"

Sam looked at his notes. "Virtualization."

"Ah. Virtualization is technical magic. It allows the new super-powerful servers being sold by Dell, IBM and other companies to be partitioned into many virtual servers inside one single physical server box. You've got one server, but the server acts like six different servers. The virtualization software controls how each of the virtual servers share the processors and memory of the one actual server."

"You know what worries me?" Sam asked. "I understand all of that."

Jake grinned and went on. "About six months back, one of our clients experienced a server malfunction. They had four physical servers supporting over forty virtual servers. Twenty were dedicated to running their EHR system. The physical server that failed was hosting six of the EHR virtual servers. The EHR system went down. This was two-thirty in the morning Sunday night."

"Don't you guys ever get any sleep?"

"Sure we do. I slept nine hours last night. But that's not an exciting story, is it?"

Sam laughed. "Okay, tell me about the exciting night."

"The Guru himself received an alert from our automated system. He woke me up to deal with this potential catastrophe. I knew that by eight o'clock, dozens of patients would start visiting our client. They'd be severely limited if their EHR system wasn't live.

"A key feature of a virtualized environment is any one of the real, physical servers can host any of the virtual servers. I connected to my client's servers using remote access, balanced the hosting of the six orphaned virtual servers among the three working real servers, and had the EHR system back on line within an hour. Never left my house! And my client didn't even know anything had happened until I emailed them with a description of the night's events."

"Cool. Still, I really hate being woken up in the middle of the night."

"We do it so you don't have to." Jake's brow furrowed and he said, almost to himself, "Wasn't that an ad for something?" He pondered that for a second, then let it go and looked up at Sam. "It's kind of like being a fireman. I was on duty that night. When the call comes in, it's my responsibility to resolve the problem - no matter what it takes."

"Better you than me."

Jake slapped Sam's shoulder. "That's exactly what I'm saying! Okay, one last thing: Disaster planning. A vital consideration in any system implementation. You back up all your data?"

"Yes," Sam lied.

"Ah. But having the data is not the same as having access to the data. I tell my clients to ask one simple question. If your system were to be totally crashed or burned, how many hours or days would it take to get the system running the way it's running today?"

Sam thought about this last point. "So if my server was to go up in smoke, I might have all my data intact on my backup, but I still wouldn't be able to use or read any of it until I got a new server."

"Exactly. How did you know this actually just happened to another Guru client? Two days before the tax filing deadline, a CPA firm called us about smoke pouring out of their server."

Sam vaguely recalled a section of The EHR Guru's website devoted to non-medical systems and software. He had ignored it.

"The smoke was coming from the motherboard. Didn't affect the hard disks, which held all their clients' tax returns. But they sure couldn't file those returns with an old, dead server. The CPA's clients would not have been very happy if those returns didn't get out on time."

"And this was two days before April fifteenth."

"Before March fifteenth," Jake corrected him. "Corporate tax filing deadline. Luckily for this CPA firm, we'd formulated a series of disaster plans for them. They activated one of them—implemented a special backup system called a TSP—Total Server Protection device."

"I've heard of this," Sam said.

"TSP allows us to not only restore any lost data, but also to run the entire downed server as a virtual server hosted inside our backup device. Within one hour, we had those accountants back up and completing tax returns. The firm was able to complete all its tax filings on time. A few days later, when their crunch was over, we installed a new server for them."

Jake flipped through his briefcase and pulled out a pamphlet. "I've given you an overview of maintenance and support. Have I missed any key concerns you have?"

"No, this is great. I appreciate that mostly you explained things in words I can understand."

Jake handed the pamphlet to Sam. "There's more info in here. A lot of the words have just one or two syllables."

Sam put the pamphlet and his notes in his briefcase. The two men stood up and shook hands.

"When's this meeting with your boss?" Jake asked

"Umm ... Tomorrow."

"Wow! You're moving quickly."

"That's why I really appreciate your time. And how everyone has been so kind to help me become better informed."

"No worries. I look forward to speaking with you again when you have more questions."

As Sam drove back to MedOne to finish off his workday, he felt as if all the information he had gathered regarding EHR systems was moving through his brain like data flowing in a well-designed network. He chuckled at his use of a technology metaphor to describe his thoughts.

He was excited about where an EHR system could take MedOne and the positive impact it would have on their company culture. But he was nervous about his ability to convey this effectively to Karen. He had been roughing out a presentation all week, adding to it as he acquired more knowledge. But show time was practically here.

Chapter 16
The Queen Returns

"SAM? SAM BUSHMAN, WHERE ARE YOU? IT'S TIME!"

Karen was back from Hong Kong. Though she loved the feeling of walking back through the doors of her own medical practice, a part of her was still in the Far East, remembering how "EHR" had become such a buzzword—buzzletters?—at the conference.

While she was away, Karen had given Sam his space. But she had exchanged emails and texts with the receptionist, Emily Hanson, so she knew Sam had been busy in her absence. Apparently, he had attended almost as many meetings as she had. As she settled in behind her desk, she found herself anticipating the meeting they were set to have. She was anxious to get it going.

*　　*　　*

"SAM!"

Sam looked up from his notes in shock. He knew that Karen's plane was landing at eight o'clock this morning, but he'd assumed she would at least stop by her house before coming in—drop off her luggage, take a shower, maybe even a quick nap. Who gets off a twenty-hour flight and comes straight to the office?

The answer, of course, was: Karen.

Sam flipped through his notes one last time. He had been up all night preparing for this meeting. Alina had helped until he finally insisted she go to bed. He had anticipated the questions Karen might ask and prepared notes regarding additional information he wanted to emphasize. He had worked through sunrise, then taken a shower, eaten a hefty breakfast, and headed in to the office. He was tired, but ready.

"Okay, I'm coming!" As he walked the few steps from his office to Karen's, Sam said a quick prayer and took a deep breath. He could not help but visualize a cliff, and himself walking closer and closer to the edge. But deep inside, he knew he was ready to fly.

*   *   *

Karen was flipping through the Guru's technology assessment report that Sam had left on her desk. She glanced up when she sensed him in her doorway. Her practice administrator looked a bit worse for wear, but confident all the same. This was a welcome change from the befuddled expression he'd had when she left for the airport two weeks earlier. As usual, Karen spoke before Sam had even reached his chair.

"It seems you took my advice and went to visit The EHR Guru."

"I've met with the EHR Guru and Dr. Taylor, like you suggested. I've also met with a number of other people over the past two weeks, and spoken to a whole bunch more on the phone. I think I've found a system that will allow us to eliminate our chart congestion problem. Not only—"

Karen stopped flipping pages and looked at Sam. "Tell me what you know that's not in this report."

Sam smiled. "What's not in there is what I've learned from doctors, nurses, and practice administrators who are using an EHR system every day to care for patients. I've even spoken with some of those patients. The night you left for Hong Kong, I did some research just to find out what 'EHR' meant."

Karen smirked. "Sam, I've been a doctor for over ten years and just attended a medical conference for the last two weeks talking about the most cutting-edge technologies in healthcare. I know what Electronic Health Records are." She opened the report again and resumed scanning.

"Yes, I realize that," Sam said. "But did the conference cover how EHRs can lower costs, reduce errors, condense patient records into one profile, and provide access to health records for doctors from any internet-capable computer anywhere in the world, even over Wi-Fi?"

Karen mumbled something.

Sam continued. "Did the conference cover how EHRs can be disaster proof? How they reduce the chance of lost patient documents, provide standardization for medical records, and contribute to an increase in overall public health?"

Karen looked up. "Sam, did I just hear you use the word, 'Wi-Fi'?"

Sam smiled. "I've learned a whole bunch of new terms these past two weeks."

"Really. Well, continue, please."

*   *   *

Sam had decided to present his information in the order in which he'd collected it, starting with his first visit to Dr. Taylor's office, the one with Kevin in tow. Karen listened intently until he mentioned the complete lack of paper on and around Tara's desk. Then her eyes moved away from him and she stared off into the distance.

"All those charts in the supply room?"

"Exactly. Gone! All gone."

Sam described the other advantages of a paperless system, such as increased appointment volume. He described the tablet computers, and how Dr. Taylor had accessed the system from his home.

"He also talked about some of the problems they had when they first installed the system."

"It became self-aware and rebelled?"

Sam smiled. "This is MedNet, not SkyNet. No, the problem was they didn't get the right training to learn how to run the system. That's when they were directed to The EHR Guru."

"Ah. I knew he would show up in this conversation eventually."

"Yeah. He may show up once or twice more."

Sam spoke for another five or ten minutes, but Karen interrupted him when he used the phrase Meaningful Use.

"I've heard the term, but tell me more," she said.

Sam wasn't sure if she really didn't know what it was, or if she did know and was testing him. Either way, he was ready for the question. He had done a lot of research since his meeting with Aviva.

"Basically, Meaningful Use is the government's way of establishing standards for the use of EHR systems. They want to make sure the systems not only benefit the practice, but also enable non-confidential data to be shared for the good of the public— tracking things like health trends, diseases, and food poisoning outbreaks. To do that, they want de-identified data uploaded to a central health exchange." If Karen was impressed with his casual use of the term de-identified, she didn't show it. "So they set a standard. If a practice buys a certified EHR system, and uses it the right way, it can qualify for incentives."

Karen got a highlighter out of her desk drawer. Sam took that as a good sign.

"And by incentives, we mean ...?"

"Money. If we qualify, the government will give us grants to implement an EHR at MedOne. For us, it could be over forty thousand dollars." He deliberately paused a moment.

"Forty K?"

"Per doctor," he added.

"I like the sound of that."

*   *   *

As Sam spoke, Karen skimmed the technology assessment report, highlighted passages, and made notes of her own. All the while, though, she was listening to everything he said.

She especially noticed the story of the fire at Taylor Pediatrics, and how they were up and running again two days later. She did a quick diagnostic in her head. If even ten percent of MedOne's files were destroyed or lost, it would be a catastrophic setback that they might not be able to recover from. Recently, a single lost chart had given her monumental headaches—literal ones that had kept her up at night. That lost chart was a major factor in her insisting Sam look into electronic record keeping.

Soon, Sam was describing his meeting with Aviva. "From a practice administrator's perspective, she highlighted so many benefits."

"Such as?"

Sam ticked them off on his fingers. "Improved first-pass pay rate. Automatic status updates regarding claims posted to our clearinghouse portal. I wouldn't have to update the superbills we submit to the clearinghouses anymore either." His fingers paused. "Doctors can automatically plug in values to the superbills during exams. You can even perform more accurate coding with the EHR's assistance during exams." That was another finger.

Karen saw a graph in her mind. The profit line was rising steadily. "Sam, I think you've caught on to something here."

*　　*　　*

Sam was engrossed in making sure the facts he was reporting came out in order—too engrossed to think about what Karen's reactions were. Two weeks of frantic research and study, two weeks of an emotional roller coaster with his livelihood and family in the balance were all being directed into a pure, focused, concentrated presentation.

"I met with the EHR Guru the next day," he said, "to review the results of the technology assessment they did of MedOne."

Karen interrupted him again. "It seems they're proposing a significant investment. I'll admit, the benefits look interesting. But it's a significant amount." She looked up at Sam. "What's their success rate getting clients to qualify for Meaningful Use?"

"One hundred percent."

"Well, that's comforting."

"Indeed." Sam held his breath for a second. "He also told me about how one of your management goals is to transform the supply room into a staff lounge."

Karen laughed out loud. "They found that? I wrote that in a memo to Emily in January, almost as a joke. It was a kind of pie-in-the-sky list I made up."

"The Guru told me that the EHR system should replace enough physical files that you may be able to achieve this goal."

Karen was speechless after that one. She just kind of looked off into the distance. Sam had never seen her speechless; he didn't know what to do. He decided to press on. "After our meeting, the Guru sent me to meet with one of his senior consultants. We discussed how to evaluate an EHR system and how to select a technology partner to assist with the implementation and support."

"Let me guess. Were they the best tech partner to utilize?"

"He actually didn't say that. But I think they may be." He told her about his meeting with Aleem, the group at Grace Presbyterian, and his discussion with Jake Carmel. And then he had nothing left to say.

They sat in silence for nearly a minute. Sam could not decipher the expression on Karen's face. Finally, he asked, "Are you alright?"

"Good," was all she said at first. "This is good." She sat back and put her hand on her mouth, like she was considering her options.

"Thank you." Sam waited. He wasn't sure what reaction he'd expected, but this certainly wasn't it.

When she made her decision, he could see it happen—in her posture, her breathing, and on her face. She smiled and turned back to Sam. "What do you recommend should be the next step for us?"

This he was prepared for. He handed her a list:

1. Distribute the EHR Guru's Technology Assessment to the other partners. (Sam has copies prepared) Ask them to review the document and write down any questions they have.

2. Schedule a meeting for The EHR Guru and possibly some of his team to walk everyone through the MedOne Tech. Assess so everyone fully understands both our current situation and where we could be.

3. Make a decision on this project within <u>one week</u> of that meeting. Our current situation is wasting too much money.

4. If we decide to a) move ahead with their recommendations and b) have The Guru's team do the work, then Karen speaks with three of their clients to confirm that our expectations for this project will be met.

Karen looked over the list. "I agree with you up to a point. But I want to talk with three of their clients now. If I become as convinced as you are, then we'll distribute copies of this tech assessment to the others and continue down your list. Are you okay with that?"

"Sounds fine to me. Would it make a difference if I disagreed?"

"Of course not," replied Karen with a smile, "but at least notice that I'm giving you an opportunity to respond. That's being respectful." The smile disappeared as quickly as it had appeared. "Are you fully convinced The EHR Guru's team is the group we should trust?"

"Yes. I haven't found anyone with more experience or greater expertise. Their rates are competitive. Their support plan is 'expensive, but worth it.' That's a direct quote from one of their clients. I spoke to people at more than a half-dozen companies who all raved about The Guru—the company and the guy. Three of them referred to The EHR Guru as their IT department. One guy even had them added to the company's phone system, so his people only have to press four digits to reach the Guru's people. They all said The EHR Guru was a partner in their business. Two of them also said they were like family."

"Did you investigate any of their competitors?"

"Yes, and I talked to some of their clients, too. Some of them said positive things, but none of them raved like the Guru's clients did."

"Okay, you get me the names and contact information of the three clients. Call the Guru and schedule a meeting with him to go over the tech assessment with our management team next week, subject to my conversations with his clients."

Sam got up from his seat. "You got it. I'll confirm via email."

He was halfway out the door when Karen brought him up short. "You know, Sam," she said. He turned to face her. "When I left on my trip, I was hoping you'd be able to suggest a couple of ways to eliminate the excess paper cluttered around the office. But you've done so much more. We're talking about eliminating paper clutter, increasing productivity, increasing revenue, and providing a better experience for our patients.

"You really impressed me today, Sam. Nice job."

Sam smiled. For once, he and Karen were on the same page. He hoped that would occur much more often in the years ahead.

The Future

Sam's tablet computer beeped at him, waking him up. He had been enjoying a fifteen-minute nap in the employee lounge. A glance at the clock told him the fifteen minutes weren't up yet.

Still a little groggy, he reached for the tablet, wondering why his break was being cut short. A "New Item Added" alert had appeared in his Schedule tab. Scrolling over, Sam clicked on the timeslot, and saw that it was a labeled as a consultation with a "Handler, Robert." Oddly, Karen had scheduled the appointment. When he saw the subject heading for what the meeting would be about, he smiled.

Sam left the lounge and headed down the hall toward Karen's office. As he knocked on the open door, he saw she was going through some patient records on her now-iconic tablet with its bright pink cover.

"I see that you scheduled me for a consult with Robert Handler?"

Karen looked up. "Sam! Yes, I did. Do you understand what it's about?"

Sam nodded. "Absolutely."

"He sounded just like you did last year. Do you need any additional—?"

"No, I have some extras."

On the way to his office, Sam used the soft-phone intercom system on his tablet to call the front office. "Emily?"

"Yes?"

"Would you please just send Robert Handler back to my office once he checks in?" He sat down at his desk and adjusted the newly mounted dinosaur picture Kevin had drawn for him.

"No problem."

"Thanks."

While Sam was reviewing some of the submitted claims in the clearinghouse portal, Joseph Eng stepped into his office.

"Hi, Sam. Just wanted to let you know we installed those latest updates on your servers."

"Wonderful! Thanks, Joe. Were there any problems? Did you have to do a reboot?"

"No, not for these. The ones that require reboots we'll do tonight after the office is closed."

"Got it. Thanks!"

"You're welcome. See ya next time."

As Joe was stepping out, a young, somewhat frazzled man almost bumped into him.

"Sorry! Excuse me," said the young man.

"No problem," said Joe, sidling around him. "Take care, Sam!"

"You too!" Sam said. He then directed his attention to the man standing in the door, motioning him in. "Hi! You must be Robert Handler, right?"

"Yes, sir. And you are Sam Bushman?"

"Guilty as charged." The two men shook hands.

"Please," said Sam, sitting back in his seat. "Sit down and get comfortable. What can I do for you?"

Robert sank into the opposite chair. "Well, long story short, I'm the administrator at a small practice in Poughkeepsie. We're drowning in paper, and I've been the one assigned to figure out how to solve it. I've heard from several people that MedOne is one of the most efficient medical groups in the area. I called today, hoping I'd get the chance to meet with someone to figure out how you do it."

"Robert," said Sam, rummaging through his desk drawer, "I think I have just what you're looking for." He handed Robert a business card and a hardcover book. Both had "The EHR Guru" printed on them. "It sounds like you are about to go on an exciting journey. Congratulations and good luck!"

Appendix
Step-by-Step: How to Implement EHR in Your Medical Practice

Doctors, medical practices and patients all suffer from the lack of easily accessible, legible, well organized, medical records and inefficient business operations. Fortunately, well designed and supported EHR systems and the technology to run these systems are available.

Following proper research, analysis and implementation project management, an EHR system enables your practice to become more efficient, organized and profitable. But there is a significant amount of work requiring a serious commitment of time and resources to insure that this journey will be successful. Stemp Systems Group can help you navigate through the challenges so you gain the most from your EHR system investment.

We wrote this parable about The EHR Guru to educate doctors and practice administrators about the benefits of Electronic Health Records in an easy, conversational way. We encourage you to join the movement towards more efficient, patient-centered, medical practices.

We are The EHR Guru.

Visit our website, www.stempsystems.com, check out our blog at wisdomforawiredworld.com or call us at (718) 784-7376 for more information. We seek to serve others by providing wisdom for a wired world.

The following pages provide a step-by-step overview of how you might start the process of implementing an EHR system in your practice.

I.   Select a Technology Partner

Investing in an EHR system is vastly different from purchasing a laptop computer. You need a technology partner that can be trusted to install, maintain, and support your EHR hardware and software components from multiple vendors 24 hours a day, seven days a week. If your personal laptop goes down, you might not have access to your home finances or family pictures for a day or two. In contrast, if your EHR system goes down, you won't have access to all your patient medical records, past medical histories, and upcoming appointments.

It is best to have professionals monitoring your system so when there is an unexpected event, they are taking immediate action to restore your access to all medical data.

Here are some actions to consider as you evaluate potential technology partners:

1. Talk with some of their clients with medical practices similar to your own.

2. Consider their years in business as a company and the experience of their team both individually, and within the organization.

3. Make certain they have worked with EHR systems for at least five years.

4. Confirm they understand the workflow of your practice.

5. Confirm their knowledge of all the requirements for Meaningful Use compliance and their experience helping clients meet these requirements.

6. Ask to see a copy of one of their EHR implementation plans.

7. Think: Do you trust them?

II. Schedule Technology Assessment

An EHR system is more than software. You also need to consider whether your current network and computers can efficiently and reliably support an EHR system. An assessment is the best way to determine the capabilities of your current technology and what upgrades are required to support your EHR implementation.

Actions Items:

1. Contact Stemp Systems Group for a free consultation to openly discuss your current environment and its challenges, if any.

2. Schedule your technology assessment.

3. Review the results of your technology assessment with senior members of our team to decide on a plan to prepare your environment to meet the technical requirements of an EHR implementation.

NOTE: The detailed technology assessment and its recommendations are a comprehensive status and planning document. While we hope you choose Stemp Systems, you are free to engage any technical partner to use this assessment and implement its recommendations.

III. Select EHR Software

Your technology assessment report provides recommendations of EHR software that have been successfully installed at similar medical practices.

Action Items:

1. Based on our discussions and a review of your technology assessment, you can decide to implement one of the software packages we recommend. If you prefer, you can invest additional time to further research alternative solutions, or engage Stemp Systems or others to do additional investigation on your behalf. This might involve:

   a. Research additional practices similar to yours to determine which EHR software they are using.

   b. Test different EHR systems. Some vendors offer trial versions that you can implement on a limited basis to consider if it is a good fit for your practice.

2. Ultimately you select and purchase the EHR software you believe is the best fit for your practice. Our job then is to assist with the project management, implementation and integration to make your EHR implementation successful and as painless as possible.

NOTE: Stemp Systems Group does not sell EHR software; therefore we do not have vendor quotas to meet. Our focus is matching your needs with the best possible technology. This is part of the reason our primary measure of success is your success.

*   *   *

Effective project management is possibly the most critical service required to successfully implement an EHR system. Most EHR vendors claim they provide all the required training and project management. This may be true to a point. Our experience shows medical practices require a strong technical resource to train people and to be available to answer questions as your staff gets acclimated to the full capabilities of your EHR technology. This person's responsibilities include serving as a project management resource to guide the entire process from planning and implementation, through go-live, and in an ongoing support role after the implementation is complete.

Some clients already have an employee who can serve as this internal resource. Many of our clients do not, so they engage Stemp as this technical resource to insure the success of their EHR implementation.

*　　*　　*

Thank you for considering the story of The EHR Guru. We are very fortunate to have served hundreds of clients who are investing their time to improve the lives of others.

Please contact us with any questions you may have or visit our website and blog for additional information.

(718) 784-7376

wisdom@stempsystems.com

www.stempsystems.com • www.wisdomforawiredworld.com

About The Authors

Morris W. Stemp
CPA, MBA, CPHIMS

Morris Stemp is a former audit manager and consultant with the firm of KPMG Peat Marwick. He is a nationally recognized expert in the areas of selection, evaluation and implementation of accounting systems. Morris Stemp has been successfully implementing integrated accounting, payroll, manufacturing and office productivity systems since 1982.

Having directed several hundred systems solution implementations in widely diverse businesses, Mr. Stemp is extremely skilled at recognizing patterns, understanding operational flows and integrating systems into existing work environments. Mr. Stemp's auditing background contributes to his ability to foresee what is required now and what will be required in the future, so that his systems solutions are complete and adaptable.

Morris Stemp has earned the designation of Certified Professional in Healthcare Information and Management Systems (CPHIMS). Already a CPA and MBA, Mr. Stemp passed a rigorous set of eligibility requirements and a certification test developed and administered by the Healthcare Information and Management Systems Society (HIMSS), demonstrating his knowledge to provide the highest level of technology expertise to healthcare organizations. He joins an elite group of fewer than 1500 certified IT professionals worldwide to earn this certification.

Morris earned a BBA in Accounting from Baruch College, summa cum laude, with a minor in Organizational Psychology and an MBA in Finance from New York University Stern School of Business.

Feel free to email Morris at mstemp@stempsystems.com.

David Russell

David Russell is CEO of Success with People, where his team trains and coaches entrepreneurs to develop a powerful company culture that provides a sustainable competitive advantage. Services include coaching, consulting, hiring/employee assessments, motivational speaking, peer groups, Best Tech Workplace surveys and programs to train companies how to deliver a more consistent superior customer experience.

He is also CEO of MANAGEtoWIN, an integrated, very low cost, online talent management portal that helps motivate people to be more productive, profitable and personally fulfilled in their careers with your company.

David has authored and co-authored five books. He has directly served over 200 organizations during the last three years. His career in the computer industry began in 1982. As a consultant, coach or speaker he has served Microsoft, Cisco, Intel, Tech Data, Ingram Micro, Autotask, ConnectWise, Tigerpaw, Catalyst Telecom, CompTIA, Heartland Technology Groups, Everything Channel, InsideNGO, Vistage and Entrepreneur's Organization members.

To learn more about David and the services he and his company provide visit:

www.SuccessWithPeople.com

www.MANAGEtoWIN.com

www.CompanyCultureChallenge.com

www.BestTechWorkplaces.com